DOING BUSINESS IN KOREA

DOING BUSINESS IN KOREA

Edited by ARTHUR M. WHITEHILL
   Professor of International Management
   College of Business Administration
   University of Hawaii

CROOM HELM
London & Sydney

NICHOLS PUBLISHING COMPANY
New York

© 1987 Korean-American Business Institute
Croom Helm Ltd, Provident House, Burrell Row,
Beckenham, Kent BR3 1AT

Croom Helm Australia, 44–50 Waterloo Road,
North Ryde, 2113, New South Wales

British Library Cataloguing in Publication Data

Doing business in Korea. — (The Croom Helm
    series in international business)
    1. Korea (South) — Economic conditions
    — 1945–
    I. Whitehill, Arthur M.
    330.9519′5043   HC467
    ISBN 0-7099-5226-0

First published in the United States of America in 1987
by Nichols Publishing Company, Post Office Box 96,
New York, NY 10024

Library of Congress Cataloging-in-Publication Data

Doing business in Korea.

    1. Korea (South) — Economic conditions — 1960-
2. Korea (South) — Commerce. 3. Investments, Foreign —
Korea (South) 4. Business etiquette — Korea (South)
I. Whitehill, Arthur M. (Arthur Murray)
HC467.D58 1987   330.9519′5043   87-5665
ISBN 0-89397-276-2

Phototypeset by Sunrise Setting, Torquay, Devon
Printed and bound in Great Britain
by Billings & Sons Limited, Worcester.

Contents

Figures and Tables

FIGURES

TABLES

Notes on Contributors

General Chang Woo Joo has had a brilliant military, business and academic career. A few of the many important positions he has held include: Dean of Faculty, National Defence College; Commanding General, 3rd Infantry Division; Senior Korean Member, UN Armistice Commission; Assistant Minister of Defence for Comptroller; Secretary General, South-North Korea Talks; President of Hyundai Corporation and of Hyundai Engineering and Construction Company; and he is currently President of the Korean-American Business Institute, which he founded in 1974.

Professor Whang Il Chung is Dean of The Business and Economics College, Hanyang University. He received his MBA from Yonsei University, and his doctorate from Washington University in the United States. He serves as Vice President, Korean Association of Small Businesses Studies, and is advisor to the Korean Chamber of Commerce, Korean Federation of Industry, Korea Employers' Federation, Esquire Shoe Company, Haitai Confectionary Manufacturing Company, Kumho Chemical Company, and many other leading organisations.

Dr Kim Kyong Dong is one of Korea's leading sociologists. After receiving his PhD from Cornell University in 1972, he taught for five years at North Carolina State University. Returning to Korea in 1977, he joined the faculty of Seoul National University where he is Professor of Sociology and Director of the Institute of Social Sciences. Recipient of many honours and awards, Professor Kim has written more than 15 books, both in Korean and English, and is the author of innumerable articles published in leading professional journals.

Dr Koo Bon Ho is presently Dean of the Graduate School and Professor of Economics at Hanyang University. He has had extensive government experience as President of the Korean Energy Research Institute and as Vice-President of the Korean Development Institute. He now serves as Co-chairman of the Financial Reform Commission, and is a member of the Monetary

Board and the Economic Planning Board. He studied for both his PhD and MA degrees at the University of Minnesota and is the author of many articles on economic and financial issues.

Dr Kim Chul Soo studied for both his MA and PhD at the University of Minnesota and is currently Assistant Minister for Trade in the Ministry of Trade and Industry, with experience in government and academic posts that spans more than two decades.

Dr Kim Soo Kon has a PhD in Industrial Relations from the University of Minnesota and an MA in Public Administration from the City University of New York. He is currently Professor and Vice Rector at the Graduate Institute of Peace Studies, Kyung Hee University; he also serves as Public Representative of the Central Labour Commission and as Chairman of the Advisory Committee on Employment and Manpower Development Policies as well as being Chairman of the National Employment Security Committee at the Ministry of Labour. Dr Kim has worked with the Korea Development Institute and the Agency for Vocational Training and Testing. He is the author of many articles dealing with industrial relations.

Dr Lee Tae Hee is Senior Partner in the Law Offices of Lee and Ko. He also holds many important positions including General Counsel, Korean Air Lines; Director, Korean Legal Centre; and Director, Seoul Bar Association. Mr Lee received the JD and LL.M degrees from Harvard Law School and the LL.M and LL.B degrees from Seoul National University. He was admitted to the Korean Bar in 1962 and the California Bar in 1976.

Dr Cho Dong Sung received his DBA degree from the Harvard Business School and his MBA from Bowling Green State University. He has received many awards, including the Ford Foundation Fellowship to study at INSEAD in France. His consulting specialities include long-term strategic planning, overseas joint ventures and general trading companies. Author of ten books on international business, he is currently Associate Professor at Seoul National University.

Jin Nyum has a BA in Economics from the College of Commerce, Seoul National University and an MA from George

Washington University. After filling various directorships at EPB, Mr Jin spent three years as Economic Counsellor for the Korean Embassy in London and assumed his present position as Assistant Minister, Economic Planning Board in 1983, having worked for the Board in several key positions for the last 25 years.

George G.B. Griffin is the Commercial Counsellor for the American Embassy in Seoul. He has filled many important posts throughout the world as a Foreign Service officer for the US Department of State and was recently South Asia Division Chief for the Department of State in Washington. He holds a BA in Political Science from the University of South Carolina.

Foreword

An important event took place in Seoul, Korea on 14th and 15th November 1985, when the first annual seminar on doing business in Korea was convened by the Korean-American Business Institute. Seventy-eight people representing 18 nations, from regions as far apart as America, Europe, Australia and the Far East gathered to learn about Korea's economy and business structures.

The country has attracted world attention as the outstanding 'fast tracker' amongst newly industrialising countries. Eclipsed until now by Japan's economic miracle, Korea's amazing growth has, until recently, been largely overlooked.

Traditionally known as the Land of the Morning Calm, the country has been anything but tranquil since the early 1960s. In a little more than 20 years, per capita GNP has risen from $87 to over $2,000, and exports have rocketed from $55 million to more than $30 billion. The world's business leaders need to look beyond Japan these days . . . to Korea.

Perhaps this was what brought the seminar participants to Korea, to hear Korea's leaders in government, business and learning discuss the Korean way of doing business.

Arthur M. Whitehill
Honolulu, Hawaii

Preface

This is the first time that a full seminar has been devoted to doing business in Korea. The programme offers a broad spectrum of lecturers from the fields associated with international business.

The Korean-American Business Institute (KABI) was founded in 1974 as a private, non-profit making institute, and operates as an independent organisation aimed at providing education, research, consultation and service support toward the advancement of mutual understanding and co-operation in the field of international business. One of KABI's strengths is cross-cultural management training that embraces the cultures of Korea, the United States, Europe and the neighbouring Asian countries.

All of us are aware of the difficulties encountered when dealing with individuals or institutions from other cultures. I recall the day I crossed the 38th parallel some 40 years ago. It was on 10 December 1945. After a long journey, I arrived at the northern bank of the Hantan river at 4.30 in the morning. I was with two other students, a man and a woman. We found nobody in the area, so we started to wade across the icy waters of the river.

Suddenly, immediately behind us, seven Russian soldiers equipped with rifles appeared from the bushes. 'You can't go south!' they said, and demanded money. We each gave them 100 Hwan, equivalent to three months expenses for college students at that time. They were not satisfied, so each of us gave 200 Hwan more. They confiscated everything of value, including my 17-jewel Japanese Seiko watch (which one of them held to his ear to make sure it worked).

They ordered us two men to go but led the girl away. When we reached the middle of the river, with water about chest high, they fired at us. Knowing we were within easy range, we turned round and raised our hands. But the Russians signalled us to continue, so we crossed the river, wading backwards until we reached the southern bank and freedom.

But now we had a new worry: American soldiers! In the Orient, 'Yankee' means 'western ghosts who sip blood', so we didn't know *what* to expect. After a mile, we spotted an American soldier. He seemed to be holding a large submachine gun, and men and women were raising and lowering their arms as they walked past him.

We thought the American would be like the Russians, and try to extort our valuables — though we had nothing left. We approached with trepidation but as we came closer, we realised that he was not holding a submachine gun but a DDT sprayer. He neither asked nor demanded anything. All we heard was 'OK' after each person was sprayed.

This, my first encounter with the West, had a great impact on my life. My notions about 'western ghosts' gave way to new concepts of human decency, justice and honour. My previous misconceptions had caused me mistrust and fear and I think this is still true for many people in the business world today.

Thus, we offer this seminar so that we all can understand each other better and rid ourselves of many of the barriers we encounter in international business.

General Chang Woo Joo

1

Doing Business with Koreans

Dr Whang Il Chung

SUMMARY

Dr Whang presents a guide to foreign businesses wishing to establish joint venture or other business relationships with Korean partners. He raises ten questions often faced by foreign managers, and suggests how to work with Korean partners.

For example, Whom do you contact first in a Korean firm? How do you reach the right person? How are decisions made? What do Koreans understand by contractual obligations? And how can you deal with the language barrier?

As Korean business expands rapidly, the number of foreign businessmen in Korea has also increased tremendously in the last 20 years. While many have achieved a good deal of success, some have not found it easy to do business in Korea, and are constantly trying to find better ways to adapt themselves to local business manners.

Those who have just started up with Korean partners tend to experience perplexing cultural differences — not only differences in language and manners, but more fundamental differences in attitudes and social norms, that make it difficult for foreign visitors to understand the Korean way of doing business. Because little is published, this chapter will attempt to provide elementary guidelines.

The views expressed are personal. They are not based on research, nor on generally accepted views of Korean business society. I have drawn on my experience as a university professor and many years as a management consultant to industrial firms in Korea, to reply to questions commonly raised by foreign

businessmen who want to do business with Koreans.
1. Whom do you contact first?
2. How do you reach the right person?
3. How should you initiate a business deal?
4. Who is likely to be the key person?
5. How are decisions usually made in standard Korean firms?
6. Are Koreans as rational as Westerners?
7. Contracts as a symbol of goodwill, not as firm agreements.
8. Will your partners keep their word?
9. How do you get to know your partners?
10. Whose language barrier: theirs or yours?

1. Whom do you contact first?

In the large firms, a visitor is usually advised to contact someone higher up, even though it is those below who will be directly responsible for the deal you have in mind. Start with the president or some other top-level executive in charge of the company.

One reason is that foreign sellers normally bring in big deals. Another is that subordinates are seldom in a position to make decisions on buying but invariably consult with their superiors. Because, in many cases, decisions are made jointly, sellers would be well advised to meet several executives in general management, procurement, plant operations or finance and to talk to them one by one.

2. How do you reach the right person?

Direct contact is less effective than mediation through a third person. Koreans feel more comfortable when they are introduced by a well-known third party. Sudden appearances are to be discouraged.

If a visitor has former business partners, he should keep these relationships alive as possible mediators for negotiations in the future, as well as for present needs. Good mediators can also be found through an alumni association, family ties, or other connections.

A prior introduction or a good mediator play such an important role that a visitor may need no appointment. He is certain to be welcomed warmly because he is already known. Self introductions or appointments made by telephone should be conducted carefully. Talking to foreigners over the phone can be highly embarrassing to a Korean, even though the language barrier has been reduced in recent years. The problem is especially severe in most small firms.

3. How should you initiate a business deal?

'Small talk' seems to be a universal phenomenon before opening up a discussion, but western visitors should take more time than they normally do and introduce themselves first. These preliminaries should reflect respect for the social distance represented by the other person's age, position and background. Social distances are more valued in Korea than in the West.

Still more care is necessary until the visitor is accepted as a friend. From the Korean businessman's viewpoint, a hurried, straightforward negotiation is usually considered impolite, and it tends to cause strain. Visitors should start with 'grounding' conversations with local executives and their mediator.

When the visitor meets a younger man in the position of director or president, the same modesty is advised. Modesty translates into respect and open-mindedness which tend to lead to success in opening a business discussion. The prevailing paternalistic ethos in business practices in Korea demand Korean manners and etiquette from the visitor. Any thinly disguised contempt, however slight, may complicate business deals.

4. Who is likely to be the key person?

When a visitor makes contact with a Korean business firm, he should look for a person who is the decision-maker. Power is exercised most strongly by owner-managers, or family-related managers, who frequently form an informal power group which is difficult for the foreigner to identify.

In most of the Korean firms employees do not, irrespective of their positions, openly resist decisions made by the owner-manager and his family. Even if such leaders make decisions beyond their formal authority, the decisions will be accepted without serious questioning.

3

5. How are decisions usually made in Korean firms?

The decision-making process is often shared. In Korean firms, the '*Pummi*' system, which is an equivalent form of consensus decision making to Japan's '*Ringi*' system, is widely adopted, though the practices may differ slightly. *Pummi* processes proposals from the lower to the upper levels of management — a vertical rather than a horizontal decision-making process. The *Ringi* system is designed to circulate proposals not only to superiors but for lateral approval and coordination among different departments.

Pummi may be used to diffuse responsibility. When documentation is the only formal evidence of jointly-made decisions, the system has been observed in form but not in substance. It is not a simple matter to define the decision-making process in general, but one-sided, top-down decision making predominates in the majority of firms in Korea.

6. Are Koreans as rational as westerners?

It is often said that the tradesmen from Kaesung, a city located just north-west of the demilitarized zone, are the only truly shrewd Korean businessmen. That implies that ordinary Korean businessmen do not understand economics, are not rational, and are not truly business minded. They are energetic and active in exploring and developing business opportunities, yet most would agree they are more intuitive than analytical, more psychological than logical.

Although such generalizations cannot be justified in all cases, the attitude of Korean managers or entrepreneurs gives ample justification in business practice for the generalization. This is particularly so in comparison with Westerners.

In most Korean firms, a higher priority is placed on the employees' loyalty and hard work than on their problem-solving ability. Behavioural factors are valued more highly than analytical skills. For example, in hiring, more weight is generally given to overall impressions than to school records.

It is important for foreign visitors to be careful not to hurt a Korean's feelings with unnecessary (in the Korean context) actions or discussion. Misunderstandings may cause far-reaching damage to an otherwise successful business relationship.

However misunderstandings, when they do happen, can also be resolved through intimate gatherings, arranged possibly with the help of a mediator.

7. Contracts as a symbol of goodwill

International business is mainly based on standardized practices which contain most of the rules governing the parties involved. A fundamental concept is the contract, which has to be honoured by all parties for business to continue. With some exceptions, Korean firms have generally been able to honour the contracts arranged with their foreign partners.

The Korean word contract is sometimes associated with an unpleasant connotation, because it implies some distrust in the opposite party. Traditionally, the integrity of a person carries more weight than a contractual promise. In such cases, a contract serves as a symbol of integrity; it is not the major element in what has been agreed upon, but an additional one. It follows that, when a contract is dishonoured, it may mean that inevitable circumstances caused it to be broken. This means that Koreans will not consider a contract as legally binding. Recontracting is a daily form of business activity and, all in all, there are fewer legal disputes than the Westerner might imagine.

Koreans' fundamentally ingrained over-optimism, and Buddhist doctrines of mercy and tolerance sometimes impair international recognition of the credibility of Korean businessmen.

8. Will your partners keep their word?

Because a contract is primarily a symbol of goodwill, it is important to help Korean partners to keep the contract. Close contact between business partners is vital. The need for extra care is not necessarily based on an assumption of lack of credibility or competence in the Korean. It is largely needed because of his inherent attitudes of excessive optimism and over-expansionism, which have been the fundamental driving forces behind the actions of Korean businessmen.

9. How do you get to know your partners

To maintain a long-lasting partnership, frequent informal gatherings between the two parties are recommended. The language barrier does not matter much. What matters is warmth and a feeling of friendship. Sometimes a surprise invitation may trigger an intimate relationship better than an expensive set dinner. The most important thing is that the two parties enjoy a family-type open-mindedness. Emotional attachment plays an important role in building up the friendship that eases the true job of doing business.

10. Whose language barrier: theirs or yours?

Even though many Korean executives receive more than six years of English teaching, only a small number actually speak it well. This language barrier raises tensions which suppress ideas, and cause Koreans to keep away.

The language barrier is not limited to vocabulary. It includes basic differences in understanding. Inadequate training in logical and analytical reasoning is a further barrier. Even differences in lifestyle. It is recommended that foreign visitors share the burden of communication and understanding in order to ease the tensions.

2

Koreans: Who are They?

Dr Kim Kyong Dong

SUMMARY

In explaining the role played by the human element and social organisation in Korea's economic success Professor Kim concludes that Korea's achievement is due to adaptability to change, supported by non-rational forces, such as the quality of human resources, to motivation and organisation.

Professor Kim does not reject the 'Confucian work ethic' explanation for Korea's technological and managerial progress but feels that education, mass communication, and other channels of information have been more important. Some Korean scholars have even stressed the negative effects of Confucian doctrines and development.

Professor Kim sees Hahn as an important psychic force in Korean behaviour — the psychological state that is caused by feelings of rancor, regret, remorse, revenge, grievances, grudge and grief.

In order to explain the unique performance of South Korea in the economic sphere over the past quarter century, I am going to focus on the human element and social organization. I will examine the motivational forces, look into the quality of human resources, and analyze the strategy of mobilization and organization. To state the conclusion first, Korea's economic achievement is a consequence of her adaptability to change, supported by various non-rational forces that have motivated and organized the people and their society.

MOTIVATION

Acculturation

Modernization of late-comer societies should be seen as a dialectical process of international acculturation and indigenous adaptation. Korea, having been a Hermit Kingdom for hundreds of years, came to experience modernization by these twin processes. The virtually forced opening of ports in the late 19th century was strongly resisted by several sectors of society.

In this first wave of acculturation, Korea failed to adapt and was annexed by the Japanese. Colonial rule meant distorted acculturation, and the native forces were again unable to make the necessary adaptive changes, because the agent for change was mainly Japanese. After liberation, the sole agent for change became the Korean people and their government. Thus far, Korea has been able to adapt fairly successfully in the economic sphere.

The important point here is that acculturation has provided both the stimulus and the information needed for change. It has opened up a new horizon, with Korea exposed to the world outside through education, mass communication and a variety of other channels. As the old Chinese saying goes, 'Seeing arouses desires!'

This, of course, is the elementary stimulus offered to any late-comer society. In the case of the Korean nation, it has also aroused a keen sense of shame and embarrassment. Korea is a nation with a long history, that was overcome by a once-barbarian neighbor now equipped with modern weaponry, organization and economic strength. It is also a country torn by civil war and shaken by a series of political turmoils. It found itself still gasping to catch up with the poor among the global community of relatively poor nations. The notion of a world system of stratification is useful to the extent that Korea, as a peripheral nation, had to crawl out from the bottom as fast as possible. The stimulus for adaptive change came largely from the process of acculturation. Acculturation also furnished the basic information required to make the necessary changes to catch up with the more advanced nations.

Insecurity and survival

One of the distinctive features of Korean history is the pattern of invasion, occupation and incessant warfare. Another characteristic has been a history of political struggle among contending groups. The nation was divided into two states with opposing ideologies, after decisions made amongst the big powers in the wake of World War Two. Unlike that other arbitrarily divided nation, Germany, the Korean nation is unique in having fought a devastating war against itself for three years. There has been no communication or exchange of people, except for very limited government-level talks, for the past generation. On top of this, there is always the threat, whether real or imaginary, of another invasion from the north.

The level of insecurity has always been high, and the value of survival as a nation-state has never been questioned. It was in the midst of political turmoil in the aftermath of violent student demonstrations in the early sixties that a military takeover restored stability. The legitimacy of the junta government was consolidated when it announced and actually carried out the first Five-Year Economic Development Plan. To overcome the sense of insecurity, the political instability, and consciousness of the rapidly modernizing world outside, the plan to build the nation-state on solid economic foundations was sufficient to stimulate people's motivation. The idea that instigation of people's insecurity may arouse their motivation has been noted as one interpretation of the Weberian psychological explanation of economic behaviour. The tension created by the insecurity needs to be released, and the psychological force emanating from the relaxation of tension may be channelled into various spheres of social behaviour. In the case of Korea, this was done in the economic realm.

Psychology of *Hahn*

A unique factor in explaining Korean behaviour is *Hahn*. There is no single English equivalent. It refers to a mixture of feelings and emotional states, including a sense of rancor, regret, remorse, revenge, grievance, grudge and grief. The feeling may be related to a gathering sense of frustration, repeated deprivation, or constant suppression of desires. A hard core of grievance

9

and rancor accumulates, which can cause both psychosomatic and psychological malaise. Released, however, it can become a tremendous psychic force.

Hahn has been widely appreciated as a distinctive characteristic of the Korean people. The nature of social-structural sources of such feelings may vary with the social status of the individual. For the nation as a whole, the state of *Hahn* has been historically accumulated because of frequent invasions and occupation. Especially strong is the emotion of *Hahn* acquired from the bitter experience of colonization by the Japanese. *Hahn* has arisen because Korea remained poor too long in spite of thousands of years of high civilization. This kind of *Hahn* feeling must have been shared by all, regardless of their social position, though most intense amongst the general populace.

For them, aspects of *Hahn* have persisted throughout history. The *Hahn* of chronic poverty is one. General poverty was caused not merely by low agricultural productivity due to poor technology but arose from severe exploitation by the traditional or colonial bureaucracy. Even after independence, bureaucratic corruption exacerbated the lack of resources and low productivity. On top of this came war, the instability in its aftermath, population explosion and urban congestion.

Political oppression, especially during the colonial period, also helped create the state of *Hahn* in the minds of Koreans. But this was eased with independence, which brought with it freedom to elect public officials, to express one's opinion, and to organize and participate in voluntary organizations. In the political realm, the more serious issue was unrestrained abuse of power on the part of those in administration and politics. The emerging upper class had an extravagant lifestyle and conspicuous consumption, leaving the impoverished masses excluded and alienated.

Another important area where the feeling of *Hahn* has been accumulating is in education and social mobility. Traditionally, these were confined to the gentry. They were closed to women and to sons of commoners and menials. Even amongst the aristocrats, illegitimate sons were barred from the government examinations that led to posts in administration or the army. No matter how gifted the individual, the door to education and status was open only to the legitimate sons of aristocrats.

During the Japanese occupation, the privileged class was restricted to the Japanese and a small minority of Koreans. When the Japanese abolished the old status system and introduced

10

general education, the door to basic education was widened in principle. In reality, only a limited number of Koreans had access to primary education, and the opportunities for secondary and higher education were even more limited. Since education was almost the only channel for mobility, the chances of any Korean without proper education moving up the ladder were restricted. Even for the better educated, the colonial system inherently imposed a ceiling.

The Korean preoccupation with education and status achievement is an expression of *Hahn*, created and hardened over generations. Once the system of universal primary schooling was established after independence, the thirst for education began to slacken. Nevertheless, for education to be effective as a channel for upwards mobility, it had to be higher education. Competition grew to enter colleges and universities. The long-cumulated *Hahn* for education and status mobility was not to be readily relaxed.

Discrimination against women has been acute in almost every aspect of life since the early days of the Yi Dynasty in Korea. Although it has been gradually eased in selective spheres, women in this country have been hardening their *Hahn* for centuries. There is a famous saying that the *Hahn* of a woman can cause frost in the middle of summer.

It was in the economic arena that the Korean people finally located the outlet to their frustration. Once released *Hahn* has turned into an enormous force inciting and motivating people to find ways to gratify their suppressed needs. It was to this deep-rooted sense of *Hahn* that the junta was able to appeal when it launched the economic development plan.

The elite too have been grinding the knife of *Hahn*, as they endured political struggles and purges. The history of political conflict in this country is full of examples of revenge between major political opponents and their factions. Those ousted from power would grow in their minds the seed of *Hahn*, waiting for the time to strike back.

Sociological studies of Korea's economic growth and modernization have pointed out that the urge for achievement and status played a central role in achieving success. *Hahn* must be the real force, though. It has so far been neglected and waits to be examined more systematically in the future.

QUALITY OF HUMAN RESOURCES

These forces alone would not have been sufficient to produce today's Korea, for people must not only be motivated but qualified. Relative to other countries around the world at similar stages of economic growth, with similar living standards, Korea possessed a well-educated population. Zeal for education has been unusually strong, and the educational system quickly expanded after independence.

Contrary to earlier stereotypes, in the 60s and 70s Koreans have proved to be industrious, aggressive and highly committed to work. A study we conducted in 1967 asked the question, 'If you had sufficient economic means to live on for the rest of your life, what would you do?'. Of the worker and manager respondents, 97.7 percent indicated they would continue working. This may be compared to a study made of Americans, in which 80 percent said Yes to the question, 'If by some chance you inherited enough money to live comfortably without working, do you think you would work anyway?'

Tenacity is another quality one would expect of a people who have been through so much and yet survived as a distinct nation. Once they have found something valuable, they will hang on to it to the end.

Koreans have demonstrated their adaptability during the current modernization. They have built something substantial almost from scratch and weathered severe storms, such as the oil shocks and natural disasters. The Korean people are usually rigid in their thought patterns, behaviour and human relations, but when it comes to survival and release of *Hahn*, they tend to move quickly to adapt to the changing environment.

Koreans have learned, in the course of a stormy history, the wisdom to wait in patience, apparently resigned but not fatalistic. Militaristic discipline has been inculcated early in life since the colonial period. Since the truce was signed in 1953, Korea has been in a state of quasi-war without a battle. To meet the challenge of invasion from the north, boys have been subjected to military or quasi-military training at school and every able young man has to serve in the army. The reserve corps is well maintained, subject to regular call ups and exercises, until men reach the age of fifty. By law, the government stages civil defence exercises every month. This kind of discipline works in Korea. It has a great deal to do with the attitude of obedience to authority, which is not based on rational or legal grounds, but on the military training and mentality inherited and buttressed over the years.

CENTRALISED AUTHORITY

Perhaps the most attractive inducement the newly installed military regime could offer was rapid economic growth. This was to give the regime legitimacy, since all it needed was to mobilise the people's support and participation in the march to prosperity. Face-saving in the world community, shedding the shameful colonial memory, and insuring security in the face of the threat from the north were the rationale for the formidable task of economic reconstruction.

People in all sectors, regions and walks of life responded to the government's call for co-operation. The government decided to maintain a guiding hand in planning, implementing and evaluating the development programmes by promoting a policy of 'guided capitalism'. This was in line with an earlier and familiar principle of social organisation in Korea. Centralised government has existed for centuries, and was only reinforced by the Japanese colonial experience. Weathering political turmoil and war, the new republic built up a strong and efficient form of government.

In the process of reconstruction from the ashes of war, entrepreneurial organisations grew fast, mainly under the influence of the United States. In 1964, there were about 9,000 enterprises employing five or more people, the total number of workers in these organisations was 563,000; the average number of employees in each enterprise was 42.8. By 1983, the average scale of enterprise decreased to 40 employees because the number of organizations had jumped to 92,000, ten times the number in 1964.

Because of the dearth of resources and shortage of capital, the government assumed primary responsibility for capital formation, resource allocation, project selection and a whole array of other activities. The private sector was not an equal partner. The Korean people are used to central government. They have experienced conscription, the Japanese programmes of general mobilisation, the wartime emergency measures, and other changes imposed by the military regime. Thus, in a way, the entire country is organized on the principle of centralised authority.

The principle of centralized authority has permeated both government and the private sector. The influence of the army should not be overlooked. The armed forces have been one of the organisations most extensively exposed to modern management, because of their involvement with the United States Forces. The political leaders who initiated the economic development plans also had military backgrounds.

The need for centralised authority may be better appreciated in light of the urgent need for rapid growth, which in turn required social and political stability. This sentiment was stated by a former prime minister:

> Some argue that wealth should be evenly distributed because of the polarization of rich and poor. But our economic capacity is still in the phase of accumulation rather than distribution. If this sort of argument spreads, people will come to hate private enterprise and the nation will stray into unrest and disorder, which we cannot afford.

CONCLUSION

I have attempted to define the Korean model of development as a form of adaptive change in the encounter with the surging tide of international acculturation and modernisation. From that perspective, I have shown that distinctive non-rational psychological forces, often uniquely experienced and defined by the Korean nation and the people, have played a significant part in helping the country succeed in the economic sphere. These forces have their roots in the nation's history. They have not only motivated the people but have led to the adoption of specific principles of organisation in order to achieve economic growth.

Neither Confucian nor Christian thought, but other forces have provided the impetus for development in Korea. Technological and management expertise have been acquired mainly through education and mass communication. Many Western observers of the economic performance of East Asia believe that neo-Confucianism must be the common thread to rapid growth. But most indigenous authors, at least in the case of Korea, doubt this and tend to stress the *negative* effects of the

Confucian tradition on modernisation and development.

I am not alone in believing that the relevance of traditional religions is slim, or at the most superficial. A virtue like discipline, for example, may not mean the same to the Confucian sage as to the political or business leader with responsibility for rapid economic growth.

The extended family is fine as long as it does not lead to favouritism, nepotism and corruption. Even if it does, it may still be all right as long as it creates loyalty. But more often than not, collectivism causes irrational management, obscures identification with larger units, and leads to factional strife. Authoritarianism has had both positive and negative effects on Korean society's performance, but even if it played a positive role during the first years of change, it may have arisen from the country's recent experiences rather than from Confucianism. As far as Korea is concerned, few believe that Confucianism has been a significant contributory factor to growth. This goes also for Buddhism and even Christianity. When it was introduced around the turn of the century, Christianity must have contributed to inculcation of democratic ideals and modern values in the minds of the younger intellectuals but there is negligible evidence that it encouraged the entrepreneurship of the 60s.

Professor Berger has pointed out that both Confucianism and Mahayana Buddhism are basically this-wordly, and suspects that the secular orientation of East Asian religions must have a significant bearing on the economic performance of the newly-industrialising countries in the region. I would be unjustified in flatly rejecting his argument but would add that in the case of Korea, shamanism, the indigenous folk religion which has influenced Korean mentality and outlook on life from time immemorial, also has a strong this-wordly tendency. Whichever world religions — Confucianism, Buddhism, Taoism or Christianity reached Korea, they became Koreanised under the influence of the shaman tradition, and evolved secular, this-wordly characteristics.

The distinctive nature of Korea's development stems from something even deeper than the secular orientation of Eastern religions. This may be a combination of the experiences of the Korean people throughout their history, and their adaptability to their changing environment, which together have produced the nation's current economic success.

Table 2.1: Stages of industrial development

	Development	Major new industries	Exports	Imports
1946–52	Foreign-aid-funded imports of finished goods	None (Korean War)		Finished consumer goods
1953–57	Development of consumer goods industry	Textiles, leather, rubber, paper, food		Capital goods and semi-finished goods
1958–61	Decline of consumer goods industry and development of manufactured goods industry	Light machines, sewing machines, electrical appliances, communications equipment, radio, fertilizers, textile machines, pulp	Consumer goods	Capital goods and semi-finished goods
1962–66	First stage of manufactured goods industry (development of industry producing semi-finished materials)	Synthetic fibers (nylon, viscose rayon, polyacrylic) fertilizers, cement, oil, PVC, automobiles	Consumer goods	Capital goods and semi-finished goods
1967–present	Second stage of manufactured goods industry (development of industry producing capital goods and semi-finished materials)	Synthetic fibers (polyester, acetate), iron and steel, electronics, automobiles, machinery, petrochemicals, shipbuilding	Consumer goods and capital goods	Capital goods

Source: *Study of the Development Process of Industrialization in Korea* (Seoul: Korean Economic Development Association, 1969)

Table 2.2: Major socio-economic indicators (1961, 1983)

	Unit	1961 A	1983 B	Ratio B/A
GNP (market price)	Billion Won	297.08	58,297.7	168.18
GNP per capita (market)	US$	82	1,880	19.8
GNP Composition	%	100.0	100.0	–
Primary industry	%	40.2	13.7	–
Secondary „	%	15.2	28.9	–
Tertiary „	%	44.6	57.4	–
Electricity generation capacity	1,000kw	367	13,115	35.7
Coal	1,000m/T	5,884	19,861	3.4
Iron and steel	„	86.9	591	6.8
Cement	„	522.9	17,650	33.8
Unemployment	%	8.1	4.1	
Schools				
Primary	–	4,700	6,500	1.4
Middle	–	1,100	2,250	2.0
High	–	600	1,500	2.5
College/University	–	58	98	1.7
Doctors	–	8,000	29,900	3.7
Televisions	1,000	31	6,960	224.5
Telephone subscribers	1,000	97	4,914	50.7
Cars	1,000	29.2	785.3	26.9
Ratio of paved road	%	14.9[a]	67.0	–
Piped water supply	%	18.5[a]	61.0	–

Note: [a] for 1963
Source: Kim (1979), Kim *et al.* (1984)

17

3

Banking and Finance

Dr Koo Bon Ho

SUMMARY

The Korean banking system began in 1878 in Pusan, when a branch of the First National Bank of Japan was opened. It was not until 1909 that the Bank of Korea became the central bank with the right to issue bank notes. Since then, the banking and financial structure in Korea has grown steadily with the establishment of a variety of commercial and industrial banks, as well as a range of non-bank financial institutions.

Major changes in the system were made in 1950 for the new Republic of Korea, when new central and general banking statutes were passed by the National Assembly. Following the military revolution of 1961, a further major reorganisation of financial institutions was undertaken.

More recently, various measures have been taken to provide a more competitive environment in financial markets. Commercial banks have been privatised and the security markets have been expanded and strengthened. Of special interest in the international field is the removal in 1985 of discriminatory restrictions on foreign branch banks. At present, there are more than 50 foreign banks operating in Korea.

The introduction of a modern banking system into Korea dates to the beginning of Japanese domination over the country. In 1878, the First National Bank of Japan opened a branch office in Pusan, the nearest port city to Japan. The bank engaged in modern banking business including the issuing of bank notes. Thereafter, Japanese banks expanded branch networks into Korea. Koreans also established banks, but most existed only briefly because of insufficient capital and lack of experience.

The Bank of Korea was founded in 1909 to function as a central bank. It took over the legal right to issue bank notes from the First National Bank which until that time had functioned as the sole bank of issue authorized by the Korean Government. After Korea was formally annexed by Japan in 1910, the Bank of Korea was renamed the Bank of Chosun in 1911 and the Korean currency replaced with new Bank of Chosun notes. Following this, numerous commercial and specialised banks were established during Japanese rule, including Chosun Industrial Bank (1918), which played a major role in medium- and long-term financing.

Prior to the Liberation, the Korean banking structure consisted of the Bank of Chosun and the Chosun Industrial Bank; two commercial banks (the Chosun Commercial Bank, later renamed the Commercial Bank of Korea, and the Choheung Bank); the Chosun Savings Bank, which was a subsidiary of the Chosun Industrial Bank and channelled its funds largely into Japanese government bonds; and the Federation of Financial Associations, which specialized in loans to farmers and small firms.

NEW BANKING SYSTEM

The sudden separation of the Korean economy from the Japanese after the Liberation in 1945 produced serious dislocation to its financial system. During the three years preceding the inauguration of the Republic of Korea in August 1948, political instability and a crippled economy created runaway inflation, which was fed by a continuously increasing money supply. Confronted with such economic disorder, the newly-established government soon recognised that the existing financial system was inadequate.

New central and general banking statutes were drafted by two executives seconded from the Federal Reserve Bank of New York, Arthur I. Bloomfield and John P. Jenson. The drafts were passed by the National Assembly in April 1950 and a new central bank, the Bank of Korea, came into being on 12th June 1950. The Bank of Korea initiated a number of policy measures to combat inflation. An institutional basis was provided for commercial banks to be reorganised under the General Banking

Act, though this was not implemented until August 1954.

The Korean War (1950–53), which broke out less than two weeks after the establishment of the Bank of Korea, created a new set of problems. After the ceasefire, the priority was to finance industrial and agricultural projects. For this purpose, the Korea Development Bank was established in 1954 with capital wholly subscribed by the government, and in 1956 the Federation of Financial Associations was reorganised into the Korea Agriculture Bank.

During the same period, commercial banks were also restructured, in order to increase funds for the short-term financing vital for economic rehabilitation. In addition to the existing commercial banks — the Choheung Bank, the Commercial Bank of Korea, and the Korea Savings Bank — the Korea Hungop Bank, later renamed the Hanil Bank, was added in 1954 through the merger of the Korea Trust Bank and the Commerce and Industry Bank. Seoul Bank was established in 1959 as a regional bank limited to Seoul and its vicinity. In 1962, the Seoul Bank was authorised to open a nationwide branch network, and later renamed the Bank of Seoul and Trust Company in 1976 when it merged with the Korea Trust Bank.

REORGANISATION

Following the military revolution of 1961, a series of measures were undertaken to promote development. The government launched the First Five Year Economic Development Plan in 1962 and reorganised the country's financial institutions in order to finance it. In 1961, a major portion of the equity capital of the commercial banks was transferred to the government and The Bank of Korea Act was amended in 1962 to strengthen government influence over the monetary policy of the Bank of Korea.

In the early 1960s, the government introduced specialised banks to facilitate financial support for underdeveloped or strategically important sectors: the National Agricultural Cooperatives Federation; the National Federation of Fisheries Cooperatives; the Small and Medium Industry Bank, and the Citizens National Bank. Later in the 1960s, the Korea Exchange Bank and the Korea Housing Bank were established. In 1983, the National Livestock Cooperatives Federation was added, to complete the present range of specialised banking institutions.

The commercial banking system was also restructured. Local banks were set up, so as to support regionally balanced development. Parallel with the rapid increase in trade volume and the internationalisation of the Korean economy, foreign banks were allowed to open branch offices in Korea.

NON-BANK FINANCIAL INTERMEDIARIES

Towards the end of the 1960s, the government recognised that the existing banking system could not meet the surging need for investment funds required for continued economic development, so it tried to diversify the sources of investment funds by introducing non-bank financial institutions and by fostering the securities market.

The Korea Development Finance Corporation, a private financial institution later renamed the Korea Long-Term Credit Bank, was incorporated to provide long-term financing. Export-Import Bank of Korea was established to facilitate financial support for exports and overseas investment. With the promulgation of the Presidential Emergency Decree in 1972, investment and finance companies were encouraged to deal in short-term debt issued by business firms. Mutual savings and finance companies were created to specialise in taking in instalment savings and extending small instalment loans. In 1974, merchant banking corporations were introduced to attract foreign capital and to supply medium- and long-term funds for business enterprises.

The securities market has also grown rapidly since 1972, supported by a series of measures to promote investment. Late in the 1970s, various institutional arrangements, such as strengthening the underwriting function of investment trust companies, and establishing the Securities and Exchange Commission and its executive body, the Securities Supervisory Board, were made to ensure the sound operation of the market.

Non-bank financial intermediaries have grown rapidly since their establishment thanks to the relatively higher interest rates they are permitted to charge. Furthermore, they enjoy a greater degree of management autonomy than the banking institutions. The market share of non-bank financial intermediaries in terms of deposits increased from 16.3 percent in 1971 to 47.3 percent in

1984. The largest increase in market share was by the investment and finance companies.

RECENT DEVELOPMENTS

The remarkable economic development of the 1960s and 1970s can be accounted for by the succession of economic development plans. Since the economy was small in scale and simple in structure, it could be controlled easily by the government. In a sense, such government control seemed to be most efficient when practised under such unfavourable conditions as limited capital stock and natural resources, large population and low national savings.

As the economy grew larger and more complex, it was felt that entrusting the management of the economy to government initiative was less efficient than entrusting it to the market mechanism. The government, therefore, shifted its policy stance in the 1980s from a government-oriented economy to one that was market-oriented. It also began to implement wide-ranging structural adjustment policies which were aimed at assigning a greater degree of reliance on the market mechanism and promoting competition in every sector of the economy.

In line with this, various measures for liberalisation and promotion of competition in the financial sector have been taken. For example, the government has privatised the four national banks: Hanil Bank in 1981, Korea First Bank and Bank of Seoul and Trust Company in 1982, and Choheung Bank in 1983. With the Commercial Bank already in private hands since 1972, the denationalisation of all five leading commercial banks was complete. The General Banking Act was revised towards the end of 1982 to give banks a freer hand in dealing with their own affairs. At the same time, their public accountability was increased by setting upper limits on the number of shares that could be held by any one body. Regulations on the internal management and operations of banks were simplified and reduced.

In order to increase their autonomy in funding, in 1982 banking institutions were given direct credit control over bank reserves. Preferential rates on policy loans by commercial banks were abolished and the bank system of loan rates, in which banks are allowed to charge different rates based on borrowers' creditworthiness, was introduced in January 1984. As a first step toward the liberalisation of interest rates, ceilings on interbank call rates and issuing rates of unsecured corporate bonds were lifted.

As a measure to provide a more competitive environment in the financial market, two new nationwide commercial banks were opened. Shinhan Bank, capitalized by Korean businessmen residing in Japan, was founded in 1982. KorAm Bank, which was underwritten by Bank of America and major companies in Korea, was opened in 1983. Entry barriers were substantially lowered for such non-bank financial institutions as investment and finance companies and mutual savings and finance companies. As a result, the number of financial institutions increased conspicuously.

Boundaries between financial institutions have become more fluid. Since 1982, the banks' ancillary business has been diversified to include the sale of commercial bills, credit card business, sales of government and public bonds on repurchase agreement (RPs), factoring, trust accounts, and certificates of deposit (CDs). In non-bank financial institutions, Commercial Paper (CP) was introduced in 1981 for investment and finance companies and merchant banking corporations, and for large securities companies in 1984. The Cash Management Account (CMA), a Korean version of MMF in the United States, was introduced in 1984 for investment and finance companies and merchant banking corporations. Finally, computerisation has enabled financial institutions to supply more sophisticated financial services such as on-line systems, cash dispensers and night depositories.

So as to encourage domestic banks to improve their banking practices and managerial skills, the government has allowed another 20 foreign banks to open branches in Korea since 1981, bringing the total of foreign banks to 52. Restrictions on foreign banks in the domestic financial market were phased out in 1985, and they were permitted to make use of rediscount facilities at the Bank of Korea for export financing and to enter the trust business. From 1986, they were entitled to make use of the rediscount facilities for all of their operations.

Liberalisation of the capital market is also underway. Two open-end investment trusts for foreign investors were opened in 1981, and a closed-end fund, called the Korea Fund, was set up in 1984. Recently three open-end trusts were added to meet the

Figure 3.1: Financial institutions

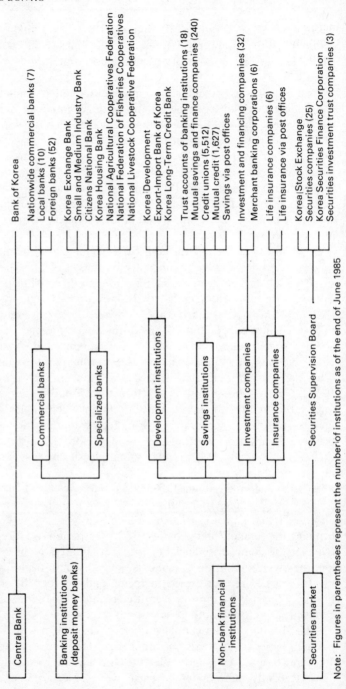

Note: Figures in parentheses represent the number of institutions as of the end of June 1985

Central Bank
- Bank of Korea

Banking institutions (deposit money banks)
- **Commercial banks**
  - Nationwide commercial banks (7)
  - Local banks (10)
  - Foreign banks (52)
- **Specialized banks**
  - Korea Exchange Bank
  - Small and Medium Industry Bank
  - Citizens National Bank
  - Korea Housing Bank
  - National Agricultural Cooperatives Federation
  - National Federation of Fisheries Cooperatives
  - National Livestock Cooperative Federation

Non-bank financial institutions
- **Development institutions**
  - Korea Development
  - Export-Import Bank of Korea
  - Korea Long-Term Credit Bank
- **Savings institutions**
  - Trust accounts of banking institutions (18)
  - Mutual savings and finance companies (240)
  - Credit unions (5,512)
  - Mutual credit (1,627)
  - Savings via post offices
- **Investment companies**
  - Investment and financing companies (32)
  - Merchant banking corporations (6)
- **Insurance companies**
  - Life insurance companies (6)
  - Life insurance via post offices

Securities market
- Securities Supervision Board
  - Korea Stock Exchange
  - Securities companies (25)
  - Korea Securities Finance Corporation
  - Securities investment trust companies (3)

24

increasing needs of foreign investors. Leading foreign securities companies now are allowed take equity in domestic securities companies, though still to a limited extent.

4

Trade Policy

Dr Kim Chul Soo

SUMMARY

Korea's successful rapid economic growth and emergence as a newly industrialised nation during the past 20 years, has been the result of sensitive responses on the part of the Korean government to changing domestic and external forces.

The deliberate shift from an import-substitution policy to export-promotion has been, in Dr Kim's judgement, the crux of Korea's successful development. Tariff exemptions, favourable financing, special tax treatment and aggressive promotion all have been used to foster exports.

Though not without its problems, the Korean experience may be instructive for other developing countries. Dr Kim stresses the essential supports for a successful export drive as: total government commitment, consistent policies, and social and economic stability.

In the past 20 years, Korea's typically agrarian society has been able to achieve rapid economic development and emerge as a newly industrialised country. Real GNP has increased sixfold since 1962. Per capital GNP has gone up from $87 in 1962 to about $2,000 in 1984.

The agricultural sector, which contributed 37 percent to the economy in 1962, had declined to 15 percent in 1984, while the share of the manufacturing sector in GNP increased from 14 percent to 31 percent during the same period.

This quantitative as well as qualitative development in Korea can be attributed to the rapid expansion of exports. In current dollars, Korea's exports grew 530 times, from $55 million in 1962 to $29,242 million in 1984.

This chapter will explore some of the reasons for the high economic growth. It will also describe how the Korean government responded to changing domestic and international circumstances in formulating Korea's trade and industrial policies over the last 20 years.

EXPORT ORIENTED DEVELOPMENT STRATEGY

It has been generally recognized that trade and industrial policies and strategies have an important bearing upon economic development. In the case of developing countries there have been two distinct sets of such policies. The first is primarily to protect domestic industries, or import substitution policies. The other relies more heavily on export promotion.[1] Experience has shown that growth has been more satisfactory under export promotion than under import substitution strategies.

During the past two decades, exports have played a vital role as engine of growth in Korea's economic development. GNP has also grown, jobs have been created and industrial production has been generated. Since 1962, Korea's strategy has been export-oriented, although elements of import substitution were present during 1972 to 1979. Therefore, one can say that an export-oriented strategy has been one of the most important factors behind Korea's success story.

There are three additional factors. First, by the time Korea launched an export-promotion policy in the early 1960s, there was already a pool of well-educated labour, and a literacy rate of 80 percent. Secondly, there was a group of highly-trained entrepreneurs who were ready to take risks. Finally, until the first oil crisis, the international economic environment was favourable. In the 1960s and the early 1970s, world trade grew nearly 8 percent annually, and the industrial countries still abided by the free trade principles of the GATT. The favourable international trading environment fostered the initial stages of the export-oriented development strategy adopted by Korea.

ROLE OF EXPORTS IN ECONOMIC DEVELOPMENT

Table 4.1 indicates the economic impact of export expansion in

Table 4.1: Impact of exports on the economy

	1975	1981	1984
1. Contribution to GNP			
GNP growth rate (%)	7.1	6.2	7.5
GNP growth rate created by exports (%)	3.9	3.0	3.8
Contribution ratio to GNP growth (%)	56.5	48.4	50.7
2. Employment			
Employment generated per $1 million exports (no. of persons)	324	101	79
Contribution ratio to overall employment (%)	13.9	15.1	15.7
3. Value-added			
Foreign exchange earnings ratio	0.65	0.63	0.63
Contribution ratio to GDP (%)	15.6	19.1	22.5
4. Production			
Production generation coefficient	1.87	2.04	2.03
Contribution ratio to production	21.9	24.1	26.2
5. Imports			
Import generation coefficient	0.35	0.36	0.37

Table 4.2: Exports by commodity

				($ million)
	1962	1976	1980	1984
Agricultural products	13	222	459	489
	(22.8%)	(2.7%)	(2.6%)	(1.7%)
Fishery products	13	519	760	878
	(22.8%)	(6.4%)	(4.3%)	(3.0%)
Mining products	16	91	136	92
	(28.1%)	(1.1%)	(0.8%)	(0.3%)
Manufactures, of which:	15	7,283	16,151	27,787
	(26.3%)	(89.8%)	(92.3%)	(95.0%)
Heavy industry	1	2,694	7,685	16,597
	(1.7%)	(33.2%)	(43.9%)	(56.9%)
Light industry	14	4,589	8,465	11,190
	(24.6%)	(56.6%)	(48.4%)	(38.3%)
Total	57	8,115	17,505	29,245

Source: Ministry of Trade and Industry

terms of economic growth, employment, income, production and imports. It shows the substantial effect of exports in all categories.

The quantitative expansion of exports since 1962 was accompanied by qualitative improvement in terms of the commodity composition of exports. In the early 1960s, minerals and agricultural products led exports; up to the mid-1970s, the main export

Table 4.3: Ratio of exports to production

	1970	1975	(%) 1980
Agriculture and fisheries	2.7	5.8	5.6
Mining products	19.8	12.4	5.5
Manufactures	10.6	18.3	19.2
Light industry	11.9	19.2	19.0
Heavy industry	7.4	17.2	19.3
Others	4.6	6.5	7.6
All sectors	6.9	12.4	13.3

Table 4.4: Contribution of exports to production, 1955–75

	Export Growth	Import Substitution	(%) Other Factors
Primary sector	22.1	−7	85.0
Manufacturing	38.0	10.7	51.4
Tertiary sector	16–17	2.5–3.0	79.8
All sectors	30.7	7.0	62.3

Source: Kwang Suk Kim (1980)

thrust was in labour-intensive light industry products; and from the mid-1970s, the export structure began to move in favour of heavy and chemical industry products (Table 4.2).

The extent export expansion has contributed to industrialization in Korea can best be seen by the ratio of exports to total production in the manufacturing sector. This ratio increased from 10.6 per cent in 1970, to 18.3 per cent in 1975, and to 19.2 per cent in 1980 (Table 4.3).

Many studies support the contention that export growth has made an important contribution to the growth of the Korean economy in general and to the manufacturing sector in particular. For example, Kwang Suk Kim finds that over the period 1955–75, export expansion contributed more to the growth of manufacturing than to that of any other sector.[2]

In 1955–63, import substitution accounted for 35 per cent of manufacturing growth while the growth of exports accounted for a little less than 11 per cent. The picture changed dramatically in the next two periods. For the period 1955–75 as a whole, export expansion made a greater contribution to the growth of manufacturing than import substitution, with 38 per cent as against 10.6 per cent (Table 4.4). More importantly, the contribution of export growth to the expansion of industrial activities was greatest in the manufacturing sector, with 38 per cent as compared with 22 per cent for the primary sector and 16 per cent or so for the tertiary sector.

CHANGING STRATEGIES

Korea's industrialisation process can be divided into four distinct phases each with a differing emphasis of trade and industrial policies and strategies.

Pre-1961

After World War Two, Korea had practically no industry: the Japanese had built their industries in North Korea and the south was principally agrarian. The Korean War destroyed about 60 per cent of what industry existed in the south. It was not until the late 1950s when nondurable consumer industries such as clothing, shoes and household goods were built for import substitution. These were followed by the rebuilding of the oil-refining industry, fertilizers, cement and plastics.

In this period, the major thrust of Korea's trade policy was to curb imports. The nation adopted a system of multiple exchange rates, in which the exchange rates applicable to private-sector imports were kept above the official exchange rate, making imports more expensive. There were also strict quantitative controls on imports, and a 'positive list' approach to imports. The import-substitution strategy reached its natural limits when the needs of the small domestic market had been met.

In the 1950s, export subsidies began to be granted. In order to offset the over-evaluation of the Won in what was principally an import-substitution regime, a system of direct export subsidies was introduced for the first time in 1954. They were repealed in 1955 but reinstated in 1961, with an export subsidy of 25 Won per dollar from 1961 to 1965. Direct export subsidies were only eliminated when the multiple exchange rates were unified in 1965.

1962–71

With the installation of the military government under President Park in 1961, economic development was made one of the major goals of the new regime. The US economic aid, which had helped to build the import-substitution industries of the earlier period, began to diminish in the early 1960s, and the government had to turn to alternative sources of foreign exchange to meet balance-of-payments difficulties. Thus in the 1962 to 1966 period, the Korean economy was restructured towards export promotion based on labour-intensive products. The policies were embodied in the First Five Year Economic Development Plan (1962–66).

Measures included a sizeable devaluation of the Won, an export-import link system, and the liberalisation and simplification of quantitative import controls. The government introduced a proliferation of administrative, tax, tariff and financial incentives between 1962 and 1965 to support exports. In 1961, for example, the government reduced corporate and personal income tax rates on export earnings by increasing the allowable deduction from 30 percent to 50 percent of such earnings.

In 1961, the government also granted tariff exemptions on raw material imports intended for the production of exports. The exemption was extended to intermediate goods and capital equipment intended for export production in 1964 and 1965. The system was changed to a tariff drawback system in the early 1970s. In 1965, the wastage allowance system was introduced, allowing exporters to import a proportion of required inputs over and above established needs. This was intended to compensate exporters for losses resulting from the proportion of imported inputs which were defective. In practice, the wastage allowance was widely used to circumvent trade restrictions on imported raw materials and intermediate goods which were not otherwise eligible. The net effect was that the system enabled some exporters to earn additional profits.

Perhaps the most important incentive was the export financing scheme, which operated through most of the 1960s and 1970s. With limited domestic capital this was an important source of credit, whose interest rates were lower than the commercial rates. The preferential rates were eliminated on 28 June 1982, when a unified interest rate structure was established.

Export promotion institutions and arrangements were established throughout the 1960s and 1970s. Among them were the

31

Export-Import Bank, a system of general trading companies and exporters associations, and the Korea Trade Promotion Corporation. After joining GATT in 1967, and under pressure from its major trading partners, the government moved away from the use of direct incentives in the early 1970s. By 1972, practically all direct incentives had been repealed or revised.

Turner and McMullen, in their study of five newly industrialising countries including Korea, concluded that the common feature of the five NICs 'is a public-policy commitment to manufactured export-oriented growth, which entails a holistic and internally consistent shift in the entire range of relevant foreign economic policies. They went on to say that, 'it is the commitment and the integrated use of various policy instruments to implement it that has enabled these countries to become significant exporters of manufactures on a global scale.'[3]

1972–79

The export-promotion strategy based on exports of labour-intensive products began to face bottlenecks in the early 1970s. Rapid wage increases weakened Korea's comparative export advantage but there was growing demand for imported parts, components, intermediate goods, and machinery and equipment.

There were at least two other international developments which caused the Korean government to reconsider export strategies in the early 1970s. One was the decision in 1971 by President Nixon to reduce US troop levels in Korea. Security concerns led Korea to develop its own defence industry. The other was protectionism by the advanced industrial countries. In 1971, for example, the US government negotiated a bilateral textile restraint agreement with Korea. At that time, textiles and apparel constituted about 40 percent of Korea's total exports. This caused Korea to diversify trading partners and to upgrade its export products to higher value-added industrial items.

The previous policy of granting easy access to imported capital goods and materials retarded the development of the domestic capital goods industry in the 1960s and the first years of the 1970s. Tariff exemptions on imported capital goods, and the financing of purchases by supplier credits with low interest rates relative to those on the domestic market, had increased the attractiveness of imported capital goods for exporters.

The upshot of these developments was the declaration by the Korean government of its heavy and chemical industrial policy in 1973. From the point of view of industrial policy, the strategy was to promote import substitution of intermediate materials and capital goods, and to promote capital-intensive industries such as shipbuilding, automobiles, iron and steel, non-ferrous metals and petrochemicals. They were labelled 'strategic industries' and given a wide variety of incentives.

The government set up three major policy vehicles to promote the heavy and chemical industries. First, it established the National Investment Fund to provide funds at preferential rates to meet large investment requirements. Two, it set up and maintained high protection for these infant industries until they could become internationally competitive. Three, it permitted monopolistic production in a number of industries so as to overcome the problems of a small domestic market.

One result was excessive investment in heavy and chemical industries at the expense of the labour-intensive light-industry sector and of small and medium business firms. During 1973–76, 71 percent of total investment in the manufacturing sector went into the heavy and chemical industries. From 1977 to 1979, this share rose to 79.1 percent. Under the preferential financing schemes made available by the government, Korean businessmen rushed into the heavy and chemical industries without regard for domestic and world demand for their products. The allocation of investment was guided less by market mechanism than by government decision. When the world economy made a downturn in the late 1970s in the aftermath of the second oil crisis, the heavy industry sector found itself with excess capacity and low utilization in most fields.

To some extent, however, the policy had worked well. The targeted industries achieved phenomenal rates of growth and led the nation to an average annual GNP growth of 10.4 percent from 1974–1979. By 1982, more than 50 percent of Korea's exports came from the industries supported by the government. Other sectors were deprived of this support and the traditional light-industry sector experienced a premature loss of competitiveness in world markets.

1980 to present

As the nation entered the 1980s, structural problems emerged which threatened further economic development. A new approach to industrial policy was called for. The most serious problem was the high rate of inflation. The nation had double digit inflation throughout the period of high growth in the 1960s and 1970s, which got worse in the latter part of the 1970s. The wholesale price index rose at an average annual rate of 20.2 percent for the period 1972–81, compared with an average 12.2 percent increase per annum for the period 1962–71; in 1980, it rose 38.9 percent over the previous year. This was attributable not only to high oil prices but also to the expansionary monetary and fiscal policies related to the policy shifts toward the heavy and chemical industries. Inflation brought with it increases in wages and other costs of production that discouraged competitiveness.

The abrupt policy shift toward the promotion of the heavy and chemical industries caused structural imbalance, particularly in investment allocation between heavy and light industries and in the share of production between large and small firms. Over the last two decades, the share of small and medium-sized industries in the manufacturing sector has declined drastically in terms of number of firms, number of employees, value of production and value added (Table 4.5).

The underdevelopment of small and medium-sized industries meant that there was no sound basis for the production of parts and components for heavy industries. This held back vertical integration within large firms, where the final products were assembled. Therefore, the heavy industries, particularly machinery and electronics, came to be characterised by a high import content of final products, which has had an adverse effect on the balance of payments.

Table 4.5: Share of small and medium-sized industries in manufacturing

	1960	1970	(%) 1979
Number of firms	99.1	96.9	96.5
Number of employees	78.1	48.4	47.5
Value of production	68.8	30.0	31.8
Value added	66.3	28.0	35.2

The currently low level of technology, particularly in the machinery and electronics sectors, has also emerged as a serious obstacle. The ratio of R & D expenditure to GNP was only 0.68 per cent in 1970. Moreover, imported technologies were often inferior and secondhand.

In the face of the worldwide economic recession that began in the late 1970s, these structural problems became more acute. After the assassination of President Park in October 1979, and the ensuing social and political instability, the economy made a sharp downturn.

Since the present government came to power in September 1980, it undertook a series of institutional reforms to restructure the economy and attain high growth and price stability, via the Revised Five Year Economic and Social Development Plan (1982–86). The strategy was to liberalise the economy both internally and externally and to introduce greater competition in all sectors by relying more on the market mechanism. In the domestic market, the government introduced competition through strong enforcement of anti-monopoly and fair trade practices. Externally, the government adopted a programme of accelerated import and foreign investment liberalisation and tariff reduction, to increase the international competitiveness of Korean products.

The government announced that the percentage of imports freed of tariffs and other constraints would be increased from 80.4 percent in 1983 to roughly 95 percent by 1988. A detailed advance-import-notice programme was also announced to give both domestic and foreign firms sufficient time to prepare themselves for the scheduled opening up of the domestic market. Tariffs were lowered from 22.6 percent in 1983 to 16.9 percent by 1988. In the field of foreign investment, a 'negative' list approach was adopted instead of the previous 'positive' list system.

The second of the revised strategies was the reform of the industrial incentive system. The role of the government in management of the economy was minimised and the role of the private sector enhanced. Government initiative was limited to those tasks which the private sector could not, or would not, undertake by itself. These include the improvement of technology by increasing investment in research and development, an encouraging attitude towards imported technology and direct foreign investment, and a programme to encourage education. Investment has also been stepped up in small and medium-sized industry and in energy conservation.

The Revised Five Year Economic and Social Development Plan set up a private sector Committee for Industrial Development to identify industries most suitable for development in the 1980s and 1990s on a selective basis, rather than the government arbitrarily picking strategic industries, as was the case in the 1970s. Thus, the new approach to industrial policy in the 1980s has been a functional incentive policy as compared to the industry-specific supports of the 1970s.

Lessons for other developing countries

It is hazardous to generalise the Korean experience for other developing countries. Nonetheless, it affirms the importance of an outward-oriented trade policy. Although this is vulnerable to external shocks, it has proved to be a better option than to look inward. It enables a country to exploit international economic opportunities, to overcome the limitations of the domestic market and to benefit from the stimulus associated with greater exposure to foreign competition.

The second lesson might be the importance of the role of the market. At the initial stages of development, the government has a definite role to play in terms of mobilising domestic and foreign resources for investment, developing infrastructure, and providing a proper business climate. But as the economy grows in size and complexity, excessive intervention by government is not a good substitute for the market mechanism, which is the better means of achieving efficient allocation of resources. The structural imbalances created in Korea's industries in the late 1970s were caused partly by arbitrary selection and special credit facilities for strategic industries.

The Korean experience also showed that social and political stability is a critical precondition for economic development. The political and social uncertainty in 1980 was, at least in part, responsible for that year's severe economic problems.

Another lesson might be that governments of developing countries should devote more resources to education and manpower development. Korea's ability to absorb new technology from abroad was remarkable precisely because of its high level of education.

Experience also indicates that economic development often neglects the healthy growth of light industries in favour of heavy industries. In the case of Korea, the industrial strategy did not specifically discourage light industries but shifted abruptly towards the heavy and chemical industries in the early 1970s. The private sector tended to invest in these new fields, neglecting investment in the traditional sector which, by then, was badly in need of product-quality upgrading.

The importance of the healthy growth of small and medium-sized enterprises to balanced development cannot be overemphasised. The parts and components-producing sector plays a crucial role in reducing the import content of assembling activities, thereby lessening the extent to which an economy has to resort to foreign debt. Besides, the promotion of the small and medium business sector has important implications for a more equitable distribution of income and the creation of a broader base of middle-income groups.

Korea's import dependency is still too high. This dependency has not decreased to any substantial degree over the last decade despite impressive growth of the overall economy. Looking back, I suspect that the Korean government has given too many incentives to exporters for too long. This has discouraged the private sector's efforts to substitute domestic production for imported intermediate goods, parts, components and capital equipment, because these were importable on preferential terms. It is difficult to judge when to reduce, or stop giving, incentives to particular activities. None the less, this does not make it any less important that the managers of an economy constantly recalculate the benefits and cost, dynamic as well as static, of any incentive system.

In conclusion, Korea's export-oriented development strategy has partly arisen from its late development, lack of natural resources, the need to trade, and a poor balance of payments. Adoption of this strategy, however, does not explain why Korea was successful in implementing it. The essential elements that seem to yield the right conditions for a sizeable and successful export drive are:

(1) Commitment by the government to an export-oriented growth strategy . . .; (2) Holistic (rather than partial) implementation of the strategy, involving consistent exchange-rate, import and export policies, and (3) Political stability to ensure the implementation of these policies over a sustained period of time.[4]

The Korean experience seems to validate this observation and may serve as a reference for other developing countries.

NOTES

1. For a discussion of the relationship between trade strategies and economic development see Anne Krueger, 'Trade Policy as an Input to Development', *The American Economic Review* (May 1980) pp. 288–92.
2. Kwang Suk Kim, *Patterns of Korea's Industrialization and the Factors* (in Korean), (Seoul, Korea Development Institute, 1980).
3. Louis Turner and Neil McMullen, *The Newly Industrializing Countries: Trade and Adjustment* (London, Royal Institute of International Affairs, 1982), p. 21.
4. Turner and McMullen, *Newly Industrializing Countries*, p. 22.

5

Labour and Employment

Dr Kim Soo Kon

SUMMARY

Korean business organisations bear striking similarities to the Japanese system, particularly their emphasis on education and seniority in compensation policies. Korea's major concern is to motivate employees and increase productivity in order to remain competitive in the global marketplace. Dr Kim recognises the important role played by technological innovation but confines his analysis to improvement in the management of human resources. For example, he cites workers' concern for job security, which is reinforced by a variety of government programmes, as a source of friction in rationalising employment and increasing productivity.

Recruitment policies, selection and promotion procedures, manpower training and development programmes are reviewed. The article closes with an analysis of current wage structures, and the criteria which determine them.

The breakthrough in productivity needed for Korean industry to compete with other developing countries can be achieved either by technological innovation or better management of human resources. Leaving the former to technical experts, this chapter discusses the latter.

LACK OF LINKAGE BETWEEN PERFORMANCE AND PAY

Wage and salary administration practices in Korea are far from

39

rational due to a number of factors such as excess labour and heavy reliance upon fringe benefits of various kinds rather than direct wages. Particularly noteworthy is that pay depends on formal education and seniority. At the time of hiring, the level of education rather than experience or position plays the major role in wage determination. As length of service increases, compensation rises regularly according to seniority. Some production workers receive various types of incentive but otherwise little consideration is given to job performance.

Because of inadequate job evaluation and superficial personnel evaluations which tend to undermine managerial authority over workers, Korean managers are handicapped in motivating workers to increase productivity. If a higher wage is paid simply to justify educational attainment or seniority, irrespective of performance, people are induced to pursue higher education rather than improve job performance. This is a serious problem particularly among white-collar workers in most Korean industries.

In spite of rapid wage increases during the late 1970s, production workers remain competitive with their counterparts in other developing countries, but this may not be true of white-collar workers due to the lack of a linkage between performance and pay.

Stability of employment

According to the Labour Standards Act, an employer is required to give at least one month's notice to a worker. The Korean government pursues a policy of employment security. Employment inspectors monitor employers' layoff practices in order to discourage them from laying off large numbers, which often leads to serious labour disputes.

There is a pervasive sentiment that employers should bear the burden of maintaining the work force, even if there is no work to be done, simply to protect its welfare. This sentiment and the government policy of employment security (employment maintenance would be a more appropriate term) have mutually reinforced each other over the years. This trend has been further strengthened in recent years by the Japan Syndrome: everything Japanese businesses do is good for labour-management relations, especially their custom of lifetime employment.

In a survey to compare Japanese and US employment practices, Whitehill and Takezawa[1] asked workers what they would expect from management if the company's business declined by 50 per cent with no sign of improvement. The question attempted to explore 'not only their (workers) perception of the proper management role but also the degree of their own willingness to accept various consequences of declining business.'[2]

The results showed that 34 percent of the US respondents and 13 percent of the Japanese workers would expect to continue working full time at normal pay as long as the company continued to exist. A more recent extension of the study to Korea shows that 56 percent of the Korean workers surveyed expect such treatment. Whereas 20 percent of the Koreans and 16 percent of the Japanese workers expected to be laid off, 27 percent of the US workers would expect likewise, which seems to reflect typical layoff practices in American industries.

A large percentage of Korean workers expected to be provided stable employment. The reason lies in Korea's economic performance during the 1970s. Twice during the decade the economy experienced recession. During the 1974 recession, a large number of small and medium-sized firms, and a few large foreign subsidiaries, laid off workers in sizeable numbers. The Office of Labour Affairs intervened and instructed the companies to inform the government two months in advance of their intention to lay off workers. This delayed and somewhat softened the impact of the layoffs.

Other companies approached the problem by offering incentives on top of normal redundancy payments, especially to female employees of marital age. Laid-off workers were mainly young girls from rural areas. Once released, many returned to the countryside and married, permanently withdrawing from the labour market.

Korea's traditional extended family system, in which the incomes of all family members are pooled, helped to ease the economic hardship of those out of work. Moreover, on government instruction, employers often rescheduled work hours rather than issue layoff notices, which forced many employers to postpone layoffs by at least a couple of months. All these factors helped to minimize the social disruption of mass unemployment and to foster workers' expectations of security. This sentiment was widely shared not only by workers but by government officials and the general public, but the result was to inhibit employment rationalisation or increases in productivity.

STAFFING AND MANPOWER DEVELOPMENT

Understanding how the labour market operates is necessary before understanding how wages are determined in Korea and evaluating the background and effects of wage guidelines. First, this section will focus upon recruitment. Second, there will be a review of selection methods and their implications for human resource management. Third, we should examine Korea's manpower development programme with special reference to skill formation.

Mode of recruitment

In the process of industrialisation the mode of recruiting employees changes, depending upon labour market conditions. During the early stages of rapid industrialisation when there was an excess of labour, a company's recruiting instrument was merely a whistle which the company's personnel manager blew to call the attention of prospective recruits living near the company gate.

As demand for labour increased during the second half of the 1970s due to rapid economic development, such recruitment methods became impractical. Recruiters were dispatched to the rural areas, where teenagers were marginally employed in agriculture. For the white-collar employees, it became common for large companies to canvass at the colleges and universities, and professors were asked to provide companies with names.

According to a Ministry of Labour survey made in 1980, almost half those hired in the preceding year found work through friends and relatives. This demonstrates that in Korea much job information is disseminated through informal channels of family ties and friends. Generally, the lower the educational level, the more likely it is that the individual will rely upon this informal channel.

The term 'open recruitment' means that jobs are obtained through individual inquiry or advertisements. About 34 percent of newly-hired employees went through these channels. The proportion of those who were assisted by the school placement office was only 3.4 percent of the total sample. The ratio tends to rise with higher education.

Only 1.2 percent of the survey sample found work through employment agencies (national employment offices under the Ministry of Labour, public employment services under local governments or private employment agencies), which demonstrates the inadequacy of Korea's formal employment services. In industrialised countries, however, one finds a similar situation; only about 10 percent of job placements are handled by public employment offices (not including private employment agencies).

Korea has 36 employment offices operated under the supervision of the Labour Ministry and seven under the supervision of local government. They all provide employment services to both employers and employees free of charge. These organisations, however, are not only understaffed, but also insufficiently motivated to do the work required of this kind of civil service. In 1970 some 33,000 job applicants were registered with the National Employment Security Office and 23,000 job openings were filed with the same organisation. Of these applicants, 10,000 were successfully placed.

Selection and promotion

Employee selection method varies significantly by industry and occupation in the Korean labour market. As has been the case in many developed countries in the past, selection procedures for lower-level personnel are not formalised. Physical checkups and examination of certificates of residence are routinely conducted but aptitude tests are rarely given, and the notion that people should be placed according to aptitude is not generally accepted.

Graduates of technical high schools or vocational training centres are usually hired through the schools' placement service. Before starting, they take a test and receive a certificate from the National Skill Test Agency. Other graduates have to pass an entrance examination or be supported by a close relative or influential friend within the firm. This kind of back door hiring was common at one time among many firms. In some ways, hiring through close relatives or friends was a good safeguard against disorder, and an effective way of protecting business secrets. In recent years, however, as the economy has become more developed and the labour market tighter, the practice has faded away.

More rigorous entrance examinations are usually given to college and university graduates. Applicants are usually tested on English proficiency and on their major field of study, such as economics or management. The examinations tend to emphasise academic performance rather than ability to fulfill the demands of the job. A predictive validation strategy at the selection stage is not yet common. At some well-organised firms, however, the corporate president himself sits in on interviews with college-graduate candidates before making the final selection.

In hiring college graduates, examination results, the prestige of the college or university, interview results and professors' recommendations are all important in the final selection. If performance in an examination rather than performance on the job becomes the basis for higher wages and promotion, this tends to block managerial motivation. Such practices reinforce the licensing function of the formal education system, especially those of the prestigious institutions of higher education. When a certificate from a formal educational institute plays such an important role, there is little incentive to take part in on-the-job training because it is no help in obtaining either a better salary or promotion.

A Westerner would be surprised at how little discretionary power a man at the middle of the organisational hierarchy enjoys with respect to hiring or firing his subordinates. Because top management relies excessively upon the personnel department, the line manager has little authority. Although the concept of line and staff is taught in many business schools, such distinctions are rarely experienced in actual organisational life. Very often a line manager must hope that whoever is referred to him from the personnel department has been thoroughly scrutinised, or accept that the applicant was referred by someone at the top or with great influence over the organisation. If an applicant is referred by someone influential, little weight is given to the line manager's opinion.

Training and development

There was little training in Korea before liberation from the

Japanese in 1945. This was because: (1) It was Japanese policy to use Korea as a supplier of raw materials for its domestic industry (2) At the time, Korea had few modern industrial plants aside from some in the textile industry (3) The Japanese permitted Koreans to occupy only low-level occupations such as labourer, once these had been vacated by the Japanese workers as they moved up the ladder. As a result, factory craft jobs were almost exclusively held by Japanese. When the Japanese left Korea, most of the factories requiring sophisticated craftsmanship remained idle for some time.

From the post-liberation era until the early 1960s, little skill formation took place mainly because of the absence of industrial development. Although private companies provided the informal training necessary to the operation of their firms, it was only after the passage of the Vocational Training Act in 1967 that a full-fledged public vocational training programme was launched. The law was enacted in response to the demand for skilled workers that was generated by the rapid industrial development that took place during the Second Five Year Economic Development Plan.

Increasingly aware of the importance of skills to the Korean economy, the government established the Central Vocational Training Institute in 1968. This trained teachers in twelve areas, including metal casting, electricity and plumbing. Between 1968 and 1980, 7,000 teachers graduated. Training institutes were then established throughout the country, totalling 24 by 1982. Current enrollment capacity is 12,400. Upon completion of training, graduates take the national skill tests to qualify as second-grade skilled workers.

Training institutes are broadly divided into three categories. The first is technical high schools, which are under the supervision of the Ministry of Education. The second is public vocational training institutes. The third is private vocational training institutes which are subdivided into (1) in-plant training centres run by employers within their own companies, and (2) non-profit private training centres.

Technical high schools and public training institutes have been the most significant contributors of skilled workers in the past. Technical education provides a broad range of skills, while vocational training emphasises more specific, immediately usable skills. Employers tend to prefer graduates of vocational training institutes to those of technical high schools because of their immediate usefulness on the job.

In order to ensure more effective co-ordination between vocational training and testing, the Korean Vocational Training and Management Agency was established in 1982 under the Ministry of Labour. Twenty-four public vocational training institutes and testing services were integrated into this agency and vocational testing is expected to be more in line with training curricula in the future.

Since the agency is not an employment service, and the National Employment Security Service is far from adequate in providing labour market information, it is doubtful whether the agency's vocational training programme can keep abreast with the changing labour market. We strongly recommend that this agency become actively involved in placement, not only for skilled but for all categories of workers. The information about the labour market that it gathers could then be used to design training programmes consistent with labour market conditions.[3]

Training in the private sector

Unlike in western industrial countries, apprenticeship programmes have not been formally introduced in Korea. Although there is an ascending hierarchical order of skilled workers ranging from trainee to semi-skilled to skilled, there is no clear delineation such as apprentice, journeyman and master.

According to the 1973 forecast of future demand for scientific and technical manpower by the Ministry of Science and Technology, an acute shortage of skilled labour was expected over the forthcoming years. This prompted the enactment in 1974 of the Special Law for Vocational Training, which required companies with 500 or more employees to offer in-plant skill training to 15 percent of the work force. In 1977, the law was expanded to include firms with 300 or more employees but reduced the training requirement to ten percent of the work force and provided an option for employers to pay a training levy within the limit of 0.25 percent of their wage bill where they were unable to provide training.

The law was hard to implement. Many companies were inadequately equipped for training. In other cases, the placement of newly-trained workers proved difficult. Some in-plant training programmes were established only so as to comply with the law. Thus, although the reported number of trainees increased rapidly after 1975, there remained concern about the substantive effect of the law.

The government's support for vocational training programmes and the enactment of compulsory training acts arose from Korea's rapid rate of industrial development. Manpower demand forecasts were made before employers recognised the possibility of shortages and made sufficient investment in human capital formation. Although compulsory vocational training, based not upon private initiative but upon the government's detailed planning was initially done with much success, the private sector lost interest in manpower development as a result.

In a country where natural resources are meagre, human resources are the only foundation on which a development strategy can be based. Korea's labour market reached a turning point in 1977–78 when the demand for skilled workers exceeded the supply, resulting in a significant increase in real wages and reduced industrial competitiveness. Regaining competitiveness is possible only through higher productivity, for which manpower development is a *sine qua non*. However, manpower development that overlooks other aspects of manpower management is bound to fail. What is needed is a comprehensive approach, encompassing not only manpower formation but also allocation, preservation and utilisation, with proper incentives and motivation (see below).

LABOUR MOBILITY

In a free labour market, economic and social benefits are the underlying force that drives workers to move from one job to another. The main reason for studying labour mobility is to evaluate the efficiency of labour markets. In general, mobility can be studied either in terms of actual movement or wish to move.

Actual worker movement may involve one or more of the following forms of mobility: inter-firm, inter-occupational, geographical or inter-industry. This section also examines severance pay in Korean industries and the results of a comparative study on worker mobility in Korea, the US and Japan.

Severance pay

Statistics of numbers leaving a company are not an exact measure of labour mobility because they ignore the difference between inter-firm movement and complete withdrawal from the labour market and also because they do not distinguish between voluntary and involuntary separation. However, in the absence of more precise data, layoff rates are acceptable to the degree that they allow inter-firm mobility and labour market fluidity to be inferred.

Whereas the average monthly separation rate for US manufacturing firms is about four percent, in Japan the rate is less than two percent and there was even a declining trend during the 1970s. Separation rates of Korean manufacturing firms are over five percent. Not only are separation rates lower in Japan, but the period of employment with a single company is longer. Studies show that twelve percent of Japanese employees have been employed at their present company for more than 20 years, while only two percent of the US workers and 0.2 percent of Korean workers have remained that long, in the 35–39 age group.

It is difficult to determine which aspects of Japanese culture are unique to their lifetime employment system, distinguishing it not only from Western but also from other Eastern countries such as Korea and China. Attributing low employee turnover rates in Japanese industries to the cultural factor alone is no help to developing countries in the process of modernisation. In search for more practical answers, an effort was made to ascertain the reasons for labour mobility among Korean manufacturing firms.[4]

Size of firm is closely related to employee turnover: the smaller a firm, the higher is the turnover. Firm size, however, is only one of several factors that are responsible for high turnover, and does not, in itself, provide a sufficient explanation.

The first quartile wage level of production workers in a firm is closely related to the separation rate. If first quartile (monthly) wages are increased by 1,000 Won, the separation rate is lower. If, therefore, a firm wants to cut high turnover in the work force, management should increase wage rates of the low-income workers. This would raise the level of the first quartile, rather than average wage of the firm.

Although there is some methodological difficulty in justifying the use of current job satisfaction to explain past turnover rate, one may assume that a firm's relative standing with regard to employee job satisfaction remains stable for some time. Judging from the highly significant regression coefficient, a strong negative association exists between average job satisfaction level of incumbent blue collar workers and separation rates.

The effect of labour unions on the turnover rate has rarely been considered, probably because of the assumption that labour unions improve wages and working conditions through monopolistic power. One study indicates that unionism reduces voluntary resignations because it plays the role of a 'a voice institution' to which workers express their discontent with management. Because of the existence of this kind of release, workers resort less often to voluntary departure. This non-wage effect of unionism on voluntary separation deserves the attention of Korean employers, who often feel that trade union activity is counterproductive and that high employee turnover is attributable to workers' lack of moral commitment or loyalty to the employer.

Finally the reducing effect of in-service training upon employee turnover is evident, though this is not determined by what kind of in-service training is offered (general skills or company specific). It is probable that investment in firm-specific human capital tends to reduce voluntary resignation. The Korean labour mobility survey suggests that claims by employers that trained workers are recruited by other companies, resulting in the loss of training expenditure, are exaggerated.

Our conclusions suggest that in order to reduce the high turnover among production workers, management should (1) raise their wage levels to be in line with those of other companies; (2) increase job satisfaction, particularly with regard to extrinsic factors; (3) permit trade unions; and (4) invest in company-specific skill training.

Propensity to move

The previous section examined actual mobility in terms of turnover rates among workers in Korea, the US and Japan. This section will examine the propensity of Korean workers to change employers, again in comparison with the US and Japan.

Whitehill and Takezawa formulated a set of questions which

they called the Cultural Continuum Checklist (the CCC scale) and administered them to US and Japanese workers. One of the CCC questionnaires examined a worker's eagerness to move if working for a declining company and offered a job with a more prosperous one.

Whitehill and Takezawa confirmed that American workers had a higher propensity to move. Of the American workers questioned, 25 percent were willing to move away from their current employer; only three percent of Japanese workers would have done so.

One might expect some similarity between Korean and Japanese industrial relations systems because of cultural characteristics shared by the two neighbouring countries. The results are quite the contrary. Although the figures fluctuate as a consequence of changing market conditions, on the whole more Korean than US workers expressed their willingness to move to another company. During the period of high labour demand in early 1979, 30 percent of Korean workers were willing to move; the percentage declined to 27 percent during the 1981 recession.

WAGE DETERMINING PROCESS

This section will review wage determining processes in the Korean labour market, primarily at the micro level. Focus will be upon firm-level factors or forces that determine wage rates and rate structures.

The first part will examine the wage structure or the composition of compensation as a means of explaining the forces of law or custom that operate in determining wages. The second section will examine the wage criteria generally accepted among Korean industries. In the third section, we discuss institutional features of the labour market which influence wage negotiation — for example, the role of workers councils in wage negotiations and the way market forces operate in the Korean labour market.

Wage rate structure

The wage system in Korea is a complex mixture of the Japanese *nenko* and the American rational system, significantly modified by Korea's employer-employee relationship and by the legal requirements of the Labour Standards Law. Even within the same industry, no two firms have the same wage rate structure, which makes comparison of wage rates between firms difficult.

Compensation can be divided into basic wage, allowances and bonuses. In general, the basic wage is the most important element. It consists of the starting wage plus annual increments and yearly base-ups. The starting salary for graduates from any school level is generally determined by the external market rate.

Annual increments are determined by age, length of service and merit. However, if employee appraisal practices are ineffective, the merit factor becomes insignificant, making age and length of service the determining factors.

The third element of the basic wage is the yearly 'base-up', usually determined by the increase in the cost of living. In an industry or occupation in which the employee's contribution is difficult to measure and does not increase in proportion to length of service, the annual increment is either a limited or an insignificant factor of wage determination. This leaves 'base-up' wage increases the main determinant of wage changes each year. This practice is far from ideal since pecuniary reward is not directly related to performance, which would be the best method to motivate employees to produce more. If the incremental portion of the basic wage is not determined in any way by the employee's performance, Korean management is seriously handicapped once a hiring decision has been made. Wages should play a dual role: income for wage earners on the one hand, and one of the most effective means of motivating the workers to produce on the other.

There are many types of allowances in the Korean wage system:

Overtime

Employers are required by Labour Standard Law to pay workers one and a half times basic wage for each additional hour worked beyond eight hours. Among many white collar occupations, an overtime allowance of two hours per day is automatically computed into monthly salary.

Late working

Employees who work during the hours from 10 pm to 6 am are entitled by law to receive one and a half times the basic wage.

Rest days

Employers are required by law to give workers one or more days off with pay each week. Employers are also required to allow one day's paid leave per month, which may be accumulated over the year.

Annual leave

Employers are required by law to allow workers eight days paid leave for one full year's service without absence, or three days leave with pay for not less than 90 percent attendance in one year's service. Also the employer is required to grant one day's paid annual leave for each consecutive year of service exceeding one year.

Menstruation and maternity

Women employees are entitled to one day's rest with pay per month and 60 days leave with pay in case of pregnancy.

These allowances are all stipulated by Labour Standard Law as minimum. Many firms also provide supplementary allowances, though they are not uniformly applied to every employee. For example, allowances for those who:

Possess skills in short supply
Hold an official skills certificate
Are assigned to remote areas
Have not missed a working day in a month or a year
Have a large number of dependants
Some firms also provide a housing allowance and/or a car allowance

As these allowances are not universally applied by every firm nor to every person in an organisation, it is difficult to measure the extent of their coverage. For an example, in the shipbuilding industry these allowances constitute about 27 percent of total pay among production workers.

The third component of employee compensation is the bonus system. Whereas allowances are usually either required by law or compensate for hardships associated with job performance, the bonus system is designed to reward workers on the basis of past performance. Since it is not required by law, the amount varies. Generally about 400 percent of monthly salary is paid in bonus in a year under normal business conditions. Often prestigious firms will continue to pay a 400 percent bonus even during recession simply to maintain their good image, though this reduces the role of the bonus as an incentive. Few small and medium-sized firms, however, can afford to pay bonuses as high as 300 or 400 percent of monthly pay in a year, so their quarterly bonuses often reflect their financial health at the time.

There is much variation among firms in the same industry group with respect to composition of basic wage, allowances and bonuses. This is due to the most controversial issue of the Korean industry's wage system, *po kwal yuck san jae*, the reverse calculation system (RCS). Korean industries devised this system in order to comply with the Labour Standard Law on allowances. Normally allowances are calculated from basic pay by multiplication of a certain ratio such as 1.5 times for overtime and another 1.5 times for late-night working hours. Under RCS, the employer agrees with his employee to pay a total monthly amount, calculated in such a way that this package meets all the allowance requirements stipulated in the law. Consequently, basic pay sometimes is nothing more than the residual remaining after calculation of all other legally required allowances.

Hence, though the composition of allowances and basic wages differs among firms, if the firms are in the same industry and competing with one another for the same labour force, the total compensation package is similar. This does not alarm either employer or employee as long as legal requirements are met since their primary concern is either total labour cost or total take-home pay.

What is significant here is that such complex wage rate structures make comparison between wages and fringe benefits difficult, and thus counter productive in motivating workers. As long as employers and employees complacently accept RCS, rationalisation of employment will be difficult to achieve, because there is no room for an hourly wage system. Because of the increasingly tight labour market brought about by sustained economic development, Korea will have to rely more heavily upon part-time employment paid on hourly basis. Unless the basic wage becomes unambiguous, no social programme covering pensions, unemployment or minimum wages, can be properly implemented.

Wage criteria

The importance people attach to wage criteria varies over time and place, by person, by industry and occupation, and according to the timing of the wage settlement. In the early stage of industrialisation, when an abundant labour supply still exists, subsistence is the highest priority. In a country of high inflation, a wage criterion such as the cost of living becomes very important.

The Korean manager's attitude toward wage criteria reveals important characteristics of the wage determination process in Korean industries. In one study, personnel managers were asked to give a percentage weight to each of the seven commonly used wage criteria. The highest weight, 18.8 percent was given to length of service, while second was to pay the going rate (17.7 percent). This may be interpreted as indicating that management places as much priority on the seniority wage system as on competitive market principles.

Equal weight percentages were given to education, performance and cost of living (14 to 15 percent). Guaranteeing subsistence was not a high priority, probably because the Korean economy had already passed through the initial take-off state in the mid-1960s and the turning point stage around 1976-77. A company's ability to pay also does not seem to influence Korean managers either. In conclusion, the starting wage is determined very much on the basis of the going rate, and increases depend foremost on length of service, followed by performance and cost of living.

Wage determining forces at micro level

In determining annual changes in wage rates at the company level, the predominant factor has been market forces, especially among small and medium-sized firms. Among the firms where a trade union has not been organised, wages and other working conditions have been determined unilaterally by the employer. However, since the passage of the Worker Council Law of 1980, firms with 30 or more employees are required to organise a worker council in which an equal number of representatives from labour and management discuss matters related to productivity and other terms of employment.

Although the right to negotiate wages is not explicitly stipulated in the law, recent practice seems to suggest that employers and employee representatives do discuss wage changes in worker councils. However, as worker councils lack the strength of labour unions, it is doubtful if they are effective in raising wages beyond what could have been obtained by market forces.

Nor have trade unions, as a social institution, on the whole been very effective in raising the level of workers' real wage rates or working conditions. Until 1981, unions were prohibited from striking by the Emergency Decree of 1972. Despite the ban, numerous disputes occurred every year, though they mostly involved issues of worker rights rather than wages and working conditions.

Union organisation is limited to a few industries, such as the long-established textile companies, and public enterprises like the railways, telecommunications and electricity, in which union members are regarded as civil servants and not permitted to strike anyway. Some of the newly emerging giant corporations are not unionised. Therefore, the unions' effectiveness in raising general wages of non-organised workers as well as their own members has been limited. However, they have been effective in providing job protection for their members, especially in the railways, ports and electricity services.

Union power, particularly at national level, has been weakened by the revision of the Labour Union Law in 1980, which was designed to promote the development of enterprise unions like those existing in Japan. Perhaps the most powerful unions in collective bargaining are the textile unions. As they have the largest membership, their federation is the pace-setter in wage and other labour-management negotiations.

The adverse effect of trade unions lies not in excessive wage demands but in corruption. This has created distrust among rank-and-file workers and led to disputes between unions.

It was not trade unions, but market forces which were responsible for the rate of real wage increases above the rate of productivity during the late 1970s.[5] It was the keen competition for college graduates among the large government-subsidised corporations in the heavy and chemical industries that exhausted the high-quality manpower pool, creating a cost-push effect on wage increases.

NOTES

1. Arthur M. Whitehill and Shin-ichi Takezawa, *The Other Worker: A Comparative Study of Industrial Relations in the United States and Japan*, (Honolulu, East-West Center Press, 1968).

2. Whitehill and Takezawa, *Other Worker*, p. 146.

3. See Soo Kon Kim, FunKoo Park and Tae Hyun Ha, *Manpower Policies for Welfare State and Employment Security* (KDI, 1981).

4. Soo Kon Kim, 'International Comparison of Separation Rates and Analysis of Their Determinants', *Korea Development Journal* (in Korean), vol. 3, no. 3, (autumn 1981) based on KDI Mobility Survey of Spring 1979.

5. Soo Kon Kim, *Wages and Labour Management Relations* (KDI, 1978).

6

Laws Governing Business

Lee Tae Hee

SUMMARY

This chapter is a legal guide to doing business in Korea and gives an overview of the laws relating to foreign business. It aims to 'suggest how to work with the system so that the system does not work against you.'

First, a general description is given of the role of government, particularly that of the Foreign Exchange Control Act. Then the options concerning form of business structure are outlined. These include: agent, representative or liaison office, branch office, partnership, limited partnership, stock company and limited liability company.

This is followed by an examination of portfolio and direct investment, tax incentives, procedures for government approval, licensing requirements and the legal aspects of sales in Korea.

The debate over protection of intellectual property — especially computer software and pharmaceutical products — is discussed. Finally, Mr Lee summarizes the labour laws likely to affect foreign business.

The Hermit Kingdom, as Korea was commonly-known to foreign traders over one hundred years ago, was known for its aversion to political, economic and cultural interchange with countries other than its geographical neighbours. More recently Korea has cast aside the mantle of seclusion and been hailed as one of the economic miracles of this century.

How did this miracle come about? What has set Korea apart from countries in which development has assumed a slower pace and more turbulent rhythm? The financial and technological

57

encouragement of the western nations, predominately the United States, cannot be over emphasised but the surge of entrepreneurial spirit that has emerged from this Hermit Kingdom, and the carefully tailored regime of stable and balanced governmental regulation, merit equal recognition.

It is the purpose of this chapter to provide a basic and practical overview of the laws and regulations of Korea related to foreign business, and to suggest how to work with the system so that the system does not work against you. Topics include how to invest or market in Korea, forms available for doing business, licensing of technology and trademarks, taxation and labour law.

ROLE OF GOVERNMENT IN ECONOMIC DEVELOPMENT

As in most other stable democracies, Koreans enjoy freedom of contract as a basic operative principal. Naturally, there are areas in which this freedom has been eroded by governmental regulations. For the most part, however, the government has limited the occurrence of such erosion to those circumstances in which parties are more than likely to contract for private gain in a manner which directly and adversely impacts upon the public good. In developed countries, the application of this principle finds expression in statutes declaring, for example, the invalidity of contracts concerning unlawful activities, as well as more business-specific laws such as anti-monopoly and anti-dumping statutes.

Perhaps paramount among these regulations is the Foreign Exchange Control Act (FECA).[1] The FECA regulates the remittance overseas of funds by residents or non-residents, the receipt of funds from abroad, and the contractual agreements which provide for such currency transactions. Residents include Korean nationals, Korean companies, including foreign companies and, in the case of individual foreigners, persons working or living in Korea for periods of six months or longer. Depending upon the transaction, the authority to issue approval is vested with the Bank of Korea, the Ministry of Finance, or any Class A foreign exchange bank. In some cases, the underlying transaction is subject to approval while in others, only the remittance of funds need be approved.

The FECA does not operate to bar remittance of funds in connection with contracts and agreements which have received the necessary approvals. Under Korean law, payment obligations are enforceable regardless of the issuance of necessary approval respecting the underlying transaction, but the remittance of the funds is contingent upon such approval. Thus, foreign parties doing business in Korea would be well advised to insist that, where necessary, approval of the underlying transaction is obtained. Then, any approval for remittance of funds in connection with the transaction will be virtually automatic.

VEHICLES FOR CONDUCTING BUSINESS AND METHODS OF INVESTMENT

A foreign party interested in conducting business in Korea must first determine the best form of business operation for the purpose. We will discuss establishing an agent relationship, representative or liaison office, branch office and the various forms of corporations. The second half of this section will focus on the methods of investing in Korean companies, including portfolio investment, wholly owned subsidiaries and joint venture companies.

Forms of entity

The choice of business structure will be a function of the type of activity the foreign party wishes to conduct in Korea and how much formal structure is required. The options listed below are ordered from the least formal to the most formal.

Agent

The easiest way for a foreign party to operate in Korea is to select a local agent. By agent, we mean an individual (either Korean or foreign) who lives in Korea and represents a foreign business. If a foreigner is selected, the agent will be responsible for his own taxes and compliance with Korean visa requirements.

The agent may only perform non-income producing activity on behalf of the principal. The agent can obtain information, perform research, and provide customer and market data. He may also buy goods or carry out advertising for the principal.

If the foreign party wants the agent to participate in sales in Korea, adverse tax consequences may result in that the foreign party might be deemed to have a permanent establishment in Korea. In other words, if the agent has authority to conclude contracts on behalf of the foreign principal, the income earned on such sales could be subject to Korean tax. In order for a foreign person to conduct tax-exempt profit-generating business activity in Korea, the Korean agent should be independent and not working for any principal. As an alternative, the Korean party could operate independently under a distribution arrangement and directly purchase the products for resale in Korea.

The principal advantage of the appointment of a local agent is the absence of formalities and the minimal cost. The foreign company, however, does not have a legal presence in Korea. The telephone, telex and bank accounts will all be in the name of the local agent. Also as the local agent should not be engaging in profit-making activities on behalf of the principal, the agent may not remit profits outside Korea.

Representative or liaison office

A representative or liaison office is similar to a local agent except that the persons working in the office are employees of the foreign company. The formalities associated with the establishment of a representative office are minimal. Although a report should be filed with the Bank of Korea (BOK) for the purpose of facilitating foreign exchange transactions, no registration with the district court or tax office is necessary. Establishment of a representative office is a simple procedure and can usually be completed in one week.

The service performed by the representative office, like that performed by a local agent, must be non income-producing liaison activities, to avoid the possibility that the foreign company would be deemed to have a permanent establishment in Korea. The representative office will not be a legal entity, and all assets of the office (including the office lease) will be in the name of the representative. Because office assets will be in the name of the individual, it is essential that he be carefully selected. This avoids disagreement regarding complete and effective transfer of such assets to a successor.

Branch office

A branch office constitutes a legal presence in Korea for the foreign company. Unlike the agent or representative, a branch can own assets and conduct business activities, including activities intended to make profits.

If the branch intends to or does, in fact, generate profit the parent company will be deemed to have a permanent establishment in Korea, thus opening the door for taxes to be assessed on all profits generated in Korea, including those profits unrelated to the activity of the local branch. In that the characterisation of permanent establishment is relevant for taxing purposes only, the actual form of business (agent, representative or liaison office, or branch office) is not considered in the determination of whether the foreign parent has a permanent establishment in Korea. Thus, individuals representing a foreign entity in Korea in either agent or liaison office form can create tax liability for the principal by exceeding the scope of authorised activity in a manner which generates profits, to the same extent as can the employees of a branch.

More specifically, the relevant statute provides that if an individual or company maintains an office or branch whose activities are limited to purchasing, arranging for third-party processing of products, storing of goods not for sale, conducting market surveys and other non profit-making activities which are essentially preparatory in nature, it will not be deemed to have a permanent establishment. By contrast, even if an individual or company does not maintain any of the establishments listed above but engages in activities such as negotiating or concluding contacts on behalf of a principal, or receiving orders or deliveries from a principal, such principal will be deemed to have a permanent establishment in Korea.

As an exception applicable to the agent form of business, it should be noted that if the agent conducts such activities for several foreign principals, then those principals will not necessarily be deemed to have a permanent establishment. Therefore, foreign companies wishing to engage in such activities without incurring tax liability are best advised to appoint an agent in Korea who represents several foreign companies rather than appointing its own exclusive agent.

Establishment of a branch requires approval of the BOK, registration with the court registration office, and registration with the local tax office. A formal application and specified list of documents must be submitted to the BOK, including a business plan identifying the type of business the branch wishes to conduct. The scope of business should be defined carefully, since a change of business carried out by the branch will require a separate application to the BOK. The regulations are not specific as to limitations of the scope of permissible branch activity.

Treatment of the application by the BOK will depend on whether the branch is seeking to remit profits from Korea. If profit remittance is requested, the BOK must 'approve' or 'deny' the application, while if profit remittance is not requested the BOK should 'accept' or 'reject' the application. In practice, the distinction between approval and acceptance is not significant. If remittance is requested, remittance of profits will be possible only three years after the date of branch establishment and, during the first five years of remittance, will be limited to 20 percent of total operating funds per annum.

The BOK's policy is not to approve branches seeking to engage in manufacture, since manufacturing operations are generally regulated by the Minister of Finance under the Foreign Capital Inducement Act. Nor can a branch engage in activities not open to foreign investment.

The branch should also register with the local district court registration office. Under Korean law, as under other legal systems, the branch manager, who may be any nationality, is empowered to contractually bind the parent company and his actions can create tort liability for the parent. Once registered with the court, the branch's legal existence begins.

Within 60 days of court registration, the branch must report its establishment to the local district tax office. The branch will be required to file regular tax returns and withhold income tax for its employees. If the branch is not deemed to be a permanent establishment, it may be possible, upon proper registration, for the branch to avoid filing returns and withholding tax. The location of the branch office must also be registered with the taxing authority.

The final requirement for a branch is to report the receipt of operating funds to the BOK. Operating funds are foreign currency capital, funds for branch establishment and funds for operating expenses sent by the head office. Receipt of initial operating funds must be reported to the BOK; BOK approval is necessary for annual operating funds in excess of US $1,000,000. Quarterly reports of the receipt of operating funds must also be filed with the BOK.

The importance of compliance with the operating funds procedures should not be overlooked. Only properly reported operating funds may be considered for calculation of profit remittance. Moreover, the regulations provide that the proceeds from liquidation of the branch may not be remitted to the extent they exceed the sum of operating funds, earned surplus and other reserves. In short, if the funds are not properly brought into Korea, difficulties will arise in removing them.

Companies

There are four types of companies recognized under Korean law as constituting separate legal entities. They are the *Hapmyung Hoesa* (partnership), *Hapcha Hoesa* (limited partnership), *Chusik Hoesa* (stock company) and *Yuhan Hoesa* (limited liability company). Korean tax authority records indicate that almost 90 percent of all Korean companies are *Chusik Hoesa*.

Neither the *Hapmyung Hoesa* nor *Hapcha Hoesa* are well suited for foreign participation. First, the law does not permit a company to become a member with unlimited liability in another company. In other words, a foreign corporation could not become a partner in a partnership or the general partner in a limited partnership. Second, there are no tax advantages to the partnership form as compared to the corporation form. The partnership, whether limited or unlimited, would still be a tax-paying entity and tax would be charged at the corporate level.

A *Yuhan Hoesa* may have only 50 members. Unlike a *Chusik Hoesa*, restrictions on transfer of share ownership are permitted. The procedure for establishing a *Yuhan Hoesa* is much simpler than those applicable to *Chusik Hoesa*. *Yuhan Hoesa* is not much used in Korea and in our experience not for foreign investors. However, in most cases of foreign-owned companies, the number of shareholders is small and restrictions on transferability of shares can legally be enforced only in a *Yuhan Hoesa*. Therefore, it may be appropriate to utilise this form in some cases.

The *Chusik Hoesa* is similar to the corporations established in the United States. The procedure of incorporation must be followed and, as with all other companies discussed, government approval must be obtained if a foreign investor is involved. Registration with the court registration office and with the local tax office is necessary.

The minimum capital of a Korean corporation is 50 million Won — thus the pure paper company is not available in Korea. Shares must have a minimum par value of 5,000 Won and cannot, except with court approval, be sold at less than par value. Restrictions on the transferability of shares, even if provided for in the articles of incorporation, will not be enforceable. However, the joint venture agreement related to the articles of incorporation often contains non-transfer provisions and liquidated damage provisions for breach of non-transfer obligations. In addition, provisions for restriction of the transfer of shares in a joint venture agreement may be enforced by injunction in the event the enforcing party learns of the contemplated transfer. Once the transfer has taken place, however, damages are the sole remedy.

Basically, all shareholders enjoy the same rights. The articles of incorporation may, however, authorise issuing of different classes of stock. These shares include preferred, non-voting, redeemable and convertible shares. Shares can be 'preferred' as to profits, interest or in the distribution of assets upon dissolution. Non-voting shares cannot exceed one fourth of total shares issued and must be preferential; this also applies to redeemable shares. For the most part, shares other than common shares have not been issued by Korean corporations, even in the case of foreign participation.

A corporation generally cannot acquire its own shares. In other words, the company would not be permitted to 'buy out' a shareholder. There are four exceptions to the general rule against a corporation acquiring its own shares: when the purchase is part of a takeover of another company; when the shares are redeemed as part of a lawful capital reduction; when a company attaches its shares through a third party in connection with legal proceedings; or when it is necessary to dispose of fractional shares. Also a more-than-40-percent-owned subsidiary cannot acquire the shares of its parent.

Corporations are managed by a board of directors. A unique aspect of a Korean corporation is the position of the representative director. Although in theory, a representative director derives his authority from the board of directors, in practice he can bind the corporation. Therefore, joint ventures with foreign parties will often have both a foreign and a Korean representative director in either joint or separate form. If joint, both signatures are required to bind the corporation. If separate, either can bind the corporation by his signature alone.

Distribution of dividends is left to the discretion of the shareholders. Corporations, however, may not distribute dividends in excess of the net assets of the company on its balance sheets less paid up capital and those reserves mandated by law (earned surplus reserves, capital surplus reserves) and voluntary reserves provided by the Articles of Incorporation or by shareholders' resolution. Dividends can be issued in the form of cash or shares, though shares are limited to 50 percent of any one dividend. Interim dividends are not permitted.

Some foreign investors have complained that their Korean counterparts refuse to vote for dividend distribution. In such cases, the cause is usually a difference of business goals. For example, the Korean party may prefer a policy of reinvestment. In other cases, the Korean party may be forbidden to distribute dividends because of the financial standing of its own or related companies. In any joint venture, company dividend policy should be resolved in advance.

INVESTMENT

We examine two methods of investment in Korea: portfolio and direct. We shall also discuss procedures for obtaining government approval and tax incentives.

Portfolio investment

At present, foreign non-residents of Korea are not permitted to acquire shares of Korean corporations on the stock exchange, except by indirect methods such as through trust funds. This is likely to change, after the announcement by the Ministry of Finance in January 1981 to open up the securities market. The plan provided for: (1) the establishment of international investment trusts permitted to acquire Korean securities by 1984; (2) limited freedom for foreign investors to invest directly in Korean securities by 1985; (3) unlimited foreign investment in Korean securities by the late 1980s; and (4) freedom for Korean securities to be listed on foreign stock exchanges and permission for capital to be allowed to leave the country by the early 1990s.

For the most part, the government has adhered to this timetable. In November 1981, the first trust funds open to foreign investment were approved. In 1984 the Korea Fund, a closed-end investment company (*i.e.* one with a fixed capitalisation of shares) listed on the New York Stock Exchange investing in Korean securities, was authorised. A similar fund based in Europe is currently being considered.

As of the time of going to press, the government had not opened the securities market to foreign investors. However, the establishment of the Korea Fund in 1984 paved the way for the nation's securities markets to be opened to international investors. When this takes place, some restrictions no doubt will be imposed upon the percentage of foreign ownership of any Korean company that will be allowed.

Direct investment and government approval

With appropriate government approval, a foreign party may establish a Korean company, either wholly-owned or in a joint venture with a Korean party, or acquire shares in an existing Korean company. Foreign investment of this type is regulated by the Ministry of Finance (MOF) under the Foreign Capital Inducement Act and regulations thereto (FCIA). In addition to the MOF, the project should be reviewed by other ministries involved and by the Economic Planning Board's Fair Trade Commission for compliance with the Monopoly Control and Fair Trade Law.

The foreign party's first concern should be whether the industry in question is open to foreign investment. Korea has adopted the negative list approach to foreign investment. If an industry is not listed on the negative list it is eligible for foreign investment. The negative list specifies 'prohibited projects' and 'restricted projects'. Approval for prohibited projects is never possible. Approval for restricted projects is possible on a case by case basis. Because government policy is to promote small and medium-sized industries, it has restricted some projects to companies which meet certain eligibility requirements. The restrictions apply to foreign investment companies, foreign investors and, where applicable, Korean joint venture partners. If the foreign investor is a 'large' company, it will only be able to invest via a joint venture with a company already engaged in the industry. The exception to the joint venture requirement is if the foreign investor intends to manufacture what Korea's existing technology is unable to produce.

There is, generally speaking, no legal limitation on the

percentage of foreign ownership allowed in any one company. In certain instances, however, Korean participation is preferred by the government. If the intended foreign participation is no more than 50 percent, the procedures for government approval are swifter.

The process begins with the submission of the application to buy plus necessary documents to the MOF. The MOF refers the matter to the ministry chiefly responsible for that industry, which carries out a feasibility study. For example, projects involving the manufacture of automobile parts are referred to the Ministry of Trade and Industry. The project is also sent to the Fair Trade Commission of the Economic Planning Board (EPB) to determine whether the agreement complies with the Monopoly Control and Fair Trade Law.

The FCIA does authorise expedited consideration of an application by the MOF without referring the application to the other ministries. To be eligible for the expedited review, the foreign investor should be seeking 50 percent of equity or less, the investment should be not more than one million US dollars, and the tax benefits pertaining to the foreign investment should be waived.

The MOF reviews comments from the ministries involved, in making its decision. Although the MOF has the authority to override a ministry veto, approval under those circumstances would be unusual. In some cases, the MOF may give conditional acceptance provided it meets certain conditions.

Conditions of approval fall into two categories. The first requires the investment to promote the domestic economy and abide by requirements for export quotas and domestic purchasing. The second condition arises in the case of a joint venture, and may request specific changes to the joint venture agreement so that it does not contain unfair provisions.

In 1981, the EPB drew on the Fair Trade Law to publish a list of guidelines affecting international contracts. With regard to joint venture agreements, the guidelines prohibit:

1. The Korean party being 'unreasonably' required to purchase raw materials or parts from the foreign investor or his designee;
2. The joint venture being required to export its products only through the foreign investor or his designee, except in cases where the foreign investor or designee is contractually

67

obligated to purchase such products at internationally reasonable prices and conditions;

3. The ratio of the number of directors the foreign investor can elect exceeding the ratio of his shareholding interest;

4. In the case of a 50-50 joint venture, giving the director elected by the foreign investor the right to break a tie;

5. Having the joint venture agreement governed by the domestic law of the foreign investor, or requiring arbitration before a body 'unfavourable' to the Korean party; and

6. Other conditions unreasonably restrictive to the Korean party and not in accordance with generally accepted international practice.

Although the approval procedure is strict, it is flexible. The foreign investor can and should take part. Prior to making any major investment, consultations should take place with the MOF, which is very willing to meet foreign investors. It is wise to remove provisions that could be viewed as over-reaching on the part of the foreign party prior to submission for approval. But if a provision is essential to the foreign investor, it may still be possible to convince the Korean government that the project is in the best interests of Korea.

The minimum initial foreign investment is US$100,000 but there is no limit on the size of subsequent injections of capital. Foreign investors may reinvest their dividends after filing a report.

Tax benefits

The Foreign Capital Inducement Act (FCIA — which is designed to 'induce', or encourage, investment of foreign capital in Korea), authorises substantial tax benefits to eligible foreign investors. Under the earlier law, tax exemptions were technically automatic, but the MOF now awards tax relief only to projects likely to significantly benefit the Korean economy. The foreign investor's request for tax relief should be made at the time of the application to the MOF for approval.

Four types of tax benefit are available. First, dividends paid to the foreign investor may be exempt from tax for any consecutive five year period within the first ten years following registration of the foreign investment company (FIC).

Second, the FIC will receive tax relief at a rate based on the percentage of the stake held by the foreign company (Foreign Investment Ratio). The FIC may either choose exemption from corporation tax under the Foreign Investment Ratio for any five year period in the first ten years following registration, or accelerated depreciation up to the amount of the investment.

Third, properties acquired by the FIC are free of tax for the first five years after registration. Finally, the following taxes are waived: customs duties, consumption tax and value added tax on capital goods used by the foreign investor in the project or purchased by the FIC with foreign capital, except in the cases of goods relating to certain industries such as agriculture, fisheries, mining, construction and insurance. If the FIC intends to purchase these goods, the purchase must be paid in foreign currency. If the intention is to repatriate the foreign currency at a later date, the investment should be retained in a foreign currency account. Custom duty exemption is automatic for all applicable investments.

Another tax saving for which all FICs are eligible concerns Korean income tax for foreign individuals working for the FIC. The Income Tax Act exempts their income from tax for five years following completion of the initial investment.

Conditions for eligibility for tax exemptions are set out in the FCIA. To be eligible, the project must make a 'significant contribution to the improvement of the international balance of payments', involve advanced technology or large amounts of capital, be carried out by non-resident nationals of Korea, be located in a free trade zone, or involve small and medium-sized industries where the Foreign Investment Ratio is less than 50 percent.

LICENSING

Licensing of foreign technology in Korea needs government approval. As with direct investment, the process is flexible and negotiation can play an important role.

When the FCIA was amended in 1984, the government approval process was changed to a reporting system, whereby reports are to be accepted or rejected within 20 days of filing unless additional time is requested for review.

When a report is filed, two government reviews are necessary.

First, the relevant ministry must approve the licence agreement. Such agreements are commonly referred to in Korea as technology assistance agreements (TAA). Second, the TAA is reviewed by the Fair Trade Commission in the FPB to see that it complies with Fair Trade Law.

The FCIA has defined the broad limitations applicable to licensing agreements. Ministries are directed not to accept TAAs which: (1) only license designs or brands; (2) are intended principally to sell raw materials, parts or accessories; (3) contain clearly unfair conditions; (4) provide low-level or out-of-date technology; or (5) involve a domestically protected industry.

Point (1) is often contested. A TAA must provide technology and not just constitute a trademark licence. Just how much technology is necessary is determined by the relevant ministry. There are numerous examples in Korea, especially in the textile industry, where the level of imported technology does not seem very high.

The ministries have developed internal policies for reviewing TAAs. From the foreign licensor's perspective, the most important policies concern the level of royalties, the method of royalty calculation, and the duration of the licensing agreement. Variations are possible but depend on convincing the authorities.

Most ministries prefer royalties not to exceed five percent. Each ministry is aware of the rates approved in similar ventures and it may be difficult to change precedent. A foreign licensor should attempt to differentiate his technology and demonstrate the relevance of the technology to Korea. The more sophisticated the technology and the more the government perceives the technology as necessary for the development of the Korean economy, the more likely it is that approval will be granted for larger royalties.

Royalties may be fixed, floating or paid up front, but the ministry must be informed of the total amounts. Except in unusual situations, royalties should be based on net sales. Net sales are determined by subtracting from gross sales the costs incurred in connection with the sales. These include sales discounts, sales returns, commissions, advertising expenses, and packing and shipping costs. Modification of the net sales formula is difficult, but possible.

The length of the licence is also determined by the ministry. Licence terms of five years are average but longer terms can be obtained. Renewal is possible.

Review by the EPB's Fair Trade Commission of the TAA to ensure that it complies with Fair Trade Law is similar to the joint venture procedures. The EPB's model licence agreement does not require review by the Fair Trade Commission. The EPB has also specified eight categories of practices to be avoided in a TAA. Before a technology assistance agreement is presented to the government for approval, provisions incorporating these practices should be deleted.

Two of the most important of the EPB prohibitions concern restrictions on export and return of the technology. Blanket restrictions on exports are not permitted. Restrictions are permitted only on a country-by-country basis and then only if the licensor regularly sells to that country, has appointed an exclusive sales agent for that country, or if sales by the Korean licensee infringe on registered industrial property rights (i.e. would infringe a patent).

A TAA may not, for the most part, require the licensee to return or cease using unregistered technology upon conclusion of the licence period. A technology licence in Korea is viewed as a technology transfer, and the licensee has rights to the unregistered technology which survive termination of the TAA. The only exceptions are if use of the technology would infringe the licensor's registered property right (i.e. a patent), or if the TAA was prematurely terminated due to breach by the licensee. Thus, careful consideration should be given to whether the length of the licence and the royalties involved justify the 'sale' of the relevant technology.

In Korean practice, licences are viewed as technical assistance agreements. The Korean licensee is expected to have obtained the necessary know-how by the end of the licensed period. Despite this, renewal is not difficult although the permitted renewal term is likely to be shorter than the original term. The licensee needs to justify the renewal, and renewal will not be permitted if its only purpose is to license a trademark.

The FCIA provides that royalty payments are exempt from Korean tax for the first five years from acceptance of the agreement, unless the exemption is waived.

TRADING LICENCES AND IMPORT REGULATIONS

Regulations relating to the import of products into Korea have recently been substantially liberalised. In this section we will examine the legal aspect of sales in Korea.

Eligible importers

Importers of products into Korea must have a trading licence issued under the Foreign Trade Transaction Act (FTTA). Several types of licence are available but the most common are general trading licences and special trading licences. Eligibility requirements for a general trading licence include paid up capital of 100 million Won. In addition one of the following must be demonstrated: initial proof of export ($200,000 or more); or manufacture of exported goods worth $300,000 or more in the previous six months; or processing of goods for a fee of $100,000 or more. To maintain the licence, which must be renewed annually, sufficient export business must be demonstrated ($500,000).

Foreign branches in Korea are eligible for special trading licences without meeting the export performance volume requirements. Under a special trading licence, the branch may import raw materials, machinery and equipment relating to certain categories of wholesale business. The products imported should be free of import restrictions and must be manufactured by the parent company of the branch or its affiliate. The imported product should be used for stock sales in Korea.

Foreign investment companies (FIC) have recently been allowed to obtain both general and special trading licences if they satisfy the basic requirements. If the FIC meets the paid up capital and export requirements for a general trading licence, the scope of its permitted import activity will depend on whether it has manufacturing facilities in Korea. If it has no manufacturing facilities, the FIC may import products that fall within eight categories of goods (which are similar to the categories allowed to branch imports) provided such products are manufactured by the FIC's parent or affiliated companies.

If the FIC has manufacturing facilities in Korea, a general trading licence authorises the FIC to import, in addition to those items importable by an FIC without manufacturing facilities, raw materials and manufacturing equipment necessary for the production of the goods it manufactures. Finally, if the FIC does not meet the requirements for a general trading licence but does have manufacturing facilities, it may import those raw materials and equipment necessary for production.

Exports of goods by holders of a trading licence are much more open. With a general trading licence, the FIC may export all freely exportable items. Those FICs having manufacturing facilities may export all products they manufacture.

The advantage of a trading licence is that import or export transactions may be consummated in the name of the branch or the FIC, which saves payment of a commission. An alternative method for participating in sales activity in Korea is for the branch or FIC to act as an offer-agent. The function of an offer-agent is to solicit orders on behalf of the principal. An offer-agent does not import in his own name and the contract of purchase is between the Korean party and the foreign party.

There are two types of offer-agents: independent and dependent. An independent offer-agent may solicit offers on behalf of anyone. To be eligible for an independent offer-agent licence, the offer-agent must have at least two representation contracts with foreign suppliers and a minimum of $30,000 in annual earned commissions. A dependent offer-agent solicits offers only on behalf of his head office and no commission minimum is required.

Two general points about offer-agents should be made. First, an offer-agent should not be able to bind his principal to a contract; if he does, the principal's income may be subject to Korean tax under the concept of permanent establishment. Second, offer-agents, especially in the case of dependent offer-agents, must earn a basic minimum commission. The taxing authority may view the claimed commission as insufficient and apply its deemed commission schedule for the purpose of imposing a higher tax.

Eligible products

Products are classified in Korea based on the Customs Cooperation Council Nomenclature (CCCN) System. The CCCN designation, which is based on industry classifications, determines not only whether a product is eligible to be imported into Korea, but what custom duties it carries.

Products for import are classified as prohibited products, restricted products and products subject to automatic approval

73

(AA). Those few products classified as prohibited may not be imported into Korea under any circumstances. If an item is designated restricted, each request to import the item must be previously approved by the relevant ministry or trade association. As noted above, the regulations related to imports have been substantially liberalised recently. As a result, the Import Liberalisation Ratio (the percentage of total number of customs categories that have been liberalised) jumped from 51.0 percent in the first half of 1977 to 68.6 percent in the second half of 1980, and then to 80.4 percent in 1983, and 87.7 percent in 1985. The government has declared its intention of increasing this ratio to 95.2 percent by 1988.

All items on the AA list may, in principle, be freely imported into Korea. If an item is AA, the importer will not need separate government approval.

Under the current liberalisation plan, a total of 7,915 items have been liberalised; of these, 6,945 are on the AA list. Restriction on their import would only be imposed if MTI decides that their effect on the domestic industry is so severe that a pre-permission requirement has to be temporarily imposed.

Another 160 items, such as tyres, synthetic dyes, vending machines etc., are still subject to a requirement of import diversification (for example, several of these items cannot be imported from Japan). The Import Diversification System is covered by Articles 21–3, Paragraph 2, Item 4 in the Trade Transaction Act and applies only to goods imported for domestic consumption.

In addition, 57 items, ranging from garlic to telephones, are subject to Import Surveillance. Import surveillance is one of the devices MTI's Import Management Committee employs to ensure harmonised liberalisation.

Imports also come under about 35 special acts which, in the past, have restricted the import of 1,973 items. This number has now been reduced to 1,600, and includes items such as certain drugs, cosmetics, arms, poisonous and radioactive substances, medicines, certain foods and household supplies, cigarettes, hemp and corn; there are also quarantine regulations for animals and plants as well as censorship regulations regarding films and disks.

At the current time, only 970 items are subject to general import restriction. MTI approval is usually subject to the recommendation of the relevant industry association designated by MTI.

In 1984, a total of 358 items including mink coats, roasted coffee, beer, domestic air conditioners, small colour TVs, vacuum cleaners, polyethylene, and special purpose trucks, were freed from import restraint. The import liberalisation ratio is expected to rise to roughly 95.2 percent by 1988. That is approximately equal to that of most advanced nations.

Customs duties

Customs duties are levied on all imported goods. The criteria are usually quality and quantity at the time of the import declaration. Particularly where the transaction is between related parties, duty is not based on invoice price but on what the customs view as the true price. The Customs Law authorises a flexible system of duties, to which up to 40 percent surcharge may be added to stabilise prices or discourage imports of particular goods.

Sellers of products into Korea should also be aware of Korea's extensive anti-dumping and countervailing duties legislation. The impact of these laws is difficult to predict, however, since no cases have been decided since the laws went into effect in January 1984.

INTELLECTUAL PROPERTY

Topics of debate

We will not attempt to summarize Korea's intellectual property laws. The country has legislation concerning the protection of patents, utility model, copyright and trademarks. There are also laws concerning unfair competition. We would like to highlight the current debate on protection for foreign intellectual property, and the US government's recent legislation on Section 301.

The debate centres on the scope and timetable of protection for foreign intellectual property. The two major areas of concern are product patents for pharmaceutical products and protection for computer software. In both cases, the Korean government has acknowledged that protection is necessary but has not deter-

75

mined when such protection will be enacted. Domestic producers strongly resist any change in legislation on the basis of the impact on domestic industry and the high demands on foreign exchange. There are strong pressures both for and against change and the solution may not be based only on legal analysis.

The Patent Act, in general, permits the issuing of product patents (protecting the substance manufactured) and process patents (protecting the method of manufacture) if eligibility requirements are met. Article 4 of the Patent Act, however, provides that inventions involving the use of chemical substances are unpatentable: the process of producing a chemical substance may be protected and not the product that results from it.

Some protection is available for computer software under the patent laws, but more substantial protection is currently under consideration. The government position is not fixed but recent announcements indicate a preference for copyright protection.

Copyright protection for foreigners

Except in the case of computer software, the distinction in the copyright laws between foreigners and non-foreigners is of importance. In general, foreign copyrights are not protected in Korea unless first publication is in Korea. Few foreign authors take advantage of the first publication exception. Legislation to grant wider protection to foreigners is under consideration.

Trademark licensing

Full trademark protection is generally available to foreigners, though the Korean Patent Office limits the scope of foreign trademark licences which are registrable. Registration of such licences is important because use of the trademark by a Korean licensee without registration may be deemed unauthorised, exposing the trademark to cancellation in a court of law. At present, in order to be registrable, trademark licences must be concluded either in connection with an approved foreign investment, an approved TAA, or the supply of raw materials by the foreign trademark owner. Amendments designed to eliminate all such regulation are currently under consideration by the Patent Office. In most cases, a trademark licence is registrable in connection with a technology assistance agreement (TAA) which has been approved under the Foreign Capital Inducement Act.

The requirement that there should be a relationship between the foreign licensor and Korean licensee (other than the trademark licence) has made franchising unaccompanied by some form of capital investment difficult. As a result, sub-licences may not be possible as there would be no privity between the foreign licensor and the Korean sub-licensee. If the sub-licensee were to use the trademarks, the foreign licensor's trademark could be subject to cancellation on the grounds that the trademark holder tacitly permitted someone to use the mark without registration of the accompanying licence. The amendments currently under consideration by the Patent Office are designed to permit franchising by eliminating the requirement of a relationship between the licensor and licensee.

The Ministry of Finance has issued a series of guidelines concerning the use of foreign trademarks in connection with TAAs. Earlier guidelines have been repealed but we believe the announcements reflect the basic policy of the government. The guidelines are important in several respects. First, they reinforce the principle that a bare trademark licence (*i.e.* a licence not in connection with a transfer of valuable technology — 'bare' of technology) is rarely permitted. Second, they set the basic provisions and scale of royalties. Third, they indicate the government intends to monitor local prices of goods bearing foreign trademarks, to be certain the prices charged are justified. One of the government's concerns is that too much is paid for the prestige of foreign trademarks.

LABOUR LAW

Labour law in Korea is relatively favourable from the foreign investor's perspective. Although some provisions are adhered to with vigour, others have not been implemented. For example, the Minister of Labour has the authority to prescribe a minimum wage for a given industry or occupation. To date, however, no minimum wage has been prescribed.

The most important statute of Korean labour law is the Labour Standards Act (LSA), which prescribes minimum requirements to improve the standard of living of workers while promoting the well-balanced development of the economy. It applies generally to any business with five or more employees. Notable features of the LSA include provisions dealing with pay and conditions of employment, redundancy, health and safety.

In theory, the LSA delegates to employer and employees broad discretion in defining rules for the work place, which are reflected in employment or collective bargaining agreements. For example, the 'normal' working week is 48 hours, usually spread over six days of eight hours, but the parties may agree to extend the working week by an additional twelve hours.

Several terms of employment are fixed. These include days-off, holiday and severance pay. Wages are often paid on a monthly, rather than hourly, basis. To avoid liability for time-and-a-half compensation, an employer should allow the employee one day a week as a 'holiday'.

Korea does not have a formal pension system, although some employers have introduced pension schemes on a company by company basis. Instead, departing employees (which includes both retirement and termination) are entitled to a severance allowance. The allowance should be at least 30 days pay for each year of employment. Employees with less than one year's service or partial years are not included.

Employees are entitled to know the reason for their dismissal. They are also entitled either to 30 days notice or 30 days pay upon leaving. Seasonal and probationary employees are excluded from this benefit.

The employer is also responsible for safety at work. He must bear the medical expenses of an employee who suffers occupational injury or disease, unless the injury occurred through the employee's gross negligence. An employee dissatisfied with pay or conditions of employment has to submit the complaint to arbitration before a lawsuit can be initiated.

Collective bargaining is authorised and protected in Korea under the Labour Union Law (LUL). Only labour unions formed according to the statutory process are entitled to recognition and protection. The articles of association, including by-laws and names of officers, must be submitted to the Minister of Labour. The Minister retains the power to cancel or amend the by-laws if he deems that they pose a threat to the public interest.

All members of the union must have a direct employment relationship with the employer. Outsiders are strictly prohibited from intervening or attempting to influence the membership in deciding upon a matter for resolution.

Unfair labour practices are defined and prohibited. Korean industry is 'open shop', because to extract from the employer a promise that all employees must join the union is forbidden. Penalising union members or organisers, refusing to bargain, subsidising the union or dismissing an employee for giving evidence concerning a violation of the law are likewise illegal. Only a labour union in good standing, however, may seek redress for an unfair labour practice, and such redress should be sought within three months of the violation.

The Labour Dispute Adjustment Law (LDAL) regulates disputes between employers and employees. Strikes (which cannot include acts of violence or subversion) are permitted but require a majority vote by the union, a report filed to the appropriate government agency and a thirty-day cooling off period. Without the proper procedures, the strike is illegal.

Another important piece of legislation is the Industrial Accident Compensation Insurance Law (IACIL). The IACIL requires employers with five or more employees to obtain insurance covering medical, lay-off, disability and funeral benefits.

The labour laws in Korea are extensive and modelled in large part on the system found in the United States, though problems sometimes arise through the lack of infrastructure to handle disputes in the work place and differences between the laws and market practice.

NOTES

1. AA; automatic approval (for import licences)
   BOK: Bank of Korea
   CCCN: Customs Cooperation Council Nomenclature
   EPB: Economic Planning Board
   FCIA: Foreign Capital Inducement Act
   FECA: Foreign Exchange Control Act
   FIC: foreign investment company
   FTTA: Foreign Trade Transaction Act
   IACIL: Industrial Accident Compensation Insurance Law
   LDAL: Labour Dispute Adjustment Law
   LSA: Labour Standards Act
   LUL: Labour Union Law
   MOF: Ministry of Finance
   MTI: Ministry of Trade and Industry
   TAA: technology assistance agreement

79

7

Government, Entrepreneurs and Competition

Dr Cho Dong Sung

SUMMARY

The difficulties faced by the Chun government since 1983 include the loss of 17 policy makers in the Rangoon bombing tragedy, high interest rates and the spread of protectionism. Korea's rapid economic progress has been underpinned by a series of Five Year Economic Plans (FYEPs), starting in 1962 and continuing with the fifth plan in 1986.

The crucial role of government is described in directing and guiding the economy and in plotting optimum strategies for long-term development. Of particular interest to foreign readers will be the description of the role of large Korean business groups known as *Chaebol*. Of the top ten groups, only one is government-owned, which may illustrate the determination of the Korean government to encourage entrepreneurship and competition as the key to continued economic growth.

In two decades, the Republic of Korea transformed its war-torn and predominantly agricultural economy into a fast-growing industrial state. Korea's real economic growth of 9.1 percent in 1983 was one of the highest in the world, and the growth rate for the remainder of the decade was projected at around seven to eight percent. Over the preceding 20 years, exports had grown at an annual rate of 34.6 percent, reaching a level of $24.2 billion in 1983 (Figure 7.1). Because Korea's economic performance was so strong, its government came under pressure to join the OECD, an organisation of 24 advanced nations for economic co-operation and development.

The growth in the Korean economy was not achieved without

Figure 7.1: Gross National Product, imports and exports, 1972–83 ($ billion)

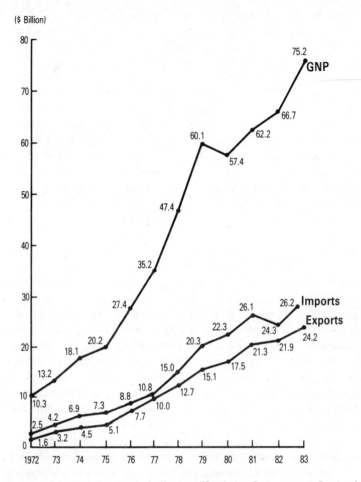

Source: Principal Economic Indicators (Statistics Department, Bank of Korea, 26.12.83), pp. 3–4

cost. There had been a rapid deterioration in the country's income distribution, which until 1975 had been judged by the World Bank to be among the most equitable in the world. The close relationship between government and big business had begun to stir the cynicism of journalists and general public, as the combined revenues of the ten largest group companies grew to account for two-thirds of Korea's gross national product. Workers with low wages started to demand their share of the pie.

In October 1979, long-time President Park Chung-Hee was assassinated by a close aide. Political turmoil followed, along with social and economic disruption. An interim civilian government gave way to military rule towards the end of 1980. Demonstrations jolted the nation as students took to the streets to demand political reform. Against the background of a world recession triggered by the second major round of oil price increases in 1979, the Korean economy experienced its worst recession in over 20 years. In 1980, GNP contracted by 6.2 percent, compared with the 9.7 percent average annual growth rate achieved during 1962–79.

By 1982, however, the Korean economy had pulled itself out of trouble. Under President Chun Doo-Hwan, a new government set out to develop a plan that would permit renewed growth, expanded exports, and greater equity in the distribution of income. The plan was based on the liberalisation of existing restrictive measures on imports, foreign investment, banking and the industrial sector. Essentially, the government was determined to reduce its direct intervention in the economy and to allow competitive market forces to bring about a more efficient allocation of resources.

As a result of this redirection of industrial policy, fixed capital formation in 1982 rose by only 11.5 percent, compared with 36.0 percent in 1978, and exports rose by only 2.8 percent, the lowest growth rate in 20 years. But for the first time in the history of Korean economic development, inflation was kept below 5 percent, down from over 35 percent in 1980 and over 20 percent in 1981.

An optimistic mood with respect to the nation's economy prevailed among Korean government policy makers throughout most of 1983, until a tragic bomb explosion in Rangoon took the lives of 17 top officials in October. Among the casualties were the chief economic adviser to the president, the deputy prime minister and minister of the Economic Planning Board, the minister of commerce and industry, and the minister of energy and resources — all prime architects of the government's liberalisation policy and major figures in its implementation.

In addition to the task of finding the right people to replace these high-calibre policy makers, President Chun Doo-Hwan had several other pressing concerns as he entered 1984, the fourth year of his seven-year term of office. The persistence of high interest rates at a time of global recession put a heavy burden on the Korean economy, the fifth largest borrower in the world, with an outstanding balance of debt of $40.6 billion. Protectionism seemed to be on the rise, especially towards Korean goods; 19 countries exercised regulatory measures against 152 import items, accounting for 22.3 percent of Korea's total exports.

Finally, President Chun's regime did not enjoy popular support among the Koreans. Political wounds caused by the financial scandal involving his wife's family in May 1982 had not completely healed. Although the Korean constitution specifically banned the re-election of any individual to the presidency, and Chun had repeatedly declared that he would not attempt to remain in office beyond his present term, rumours persisted that his political followers might attempt to amend the constitution to allow him to succeed himself.

ECONOMY

Korea's rapid economic progress over the past 20 years was all the more impressive in light of the destruction left by the war, its high population density, its lack of natural resources and its need to maintain one of the world's largest military forces. Much of the difficulty stemmed from the division of the Korean peninsula in 1945. North Korea inherited most of the mineral and hydroelectric resources and most of the existing heavy industrial base previously built by the Japanese. The Republic of South Korea was left with a large unskilled labour pool and most of the peninsula's limited agricultural resources. A large influx of refugees from North Korea added to the South's economic woes. In 1962, South Korea's per capita GNP stood at $87 per annum, far below that of the North.

Korea's industrial growth began in the early 1960s, when the Park government instituted a series of five year economic plans (FYEPs) (Table 7.1).

Table 7.1: Five year economic plans, 1962–86

FYEP	Period	GNP Per annum growth target	GNP Average actual growth	Export Five-year actual growth	Major goals
1st	1962–66	7.1%	7.8%	45.7%	Import substitution, creation of infra-structure
2nd	1967–71	7.0%	9.7%	39.3%	Export industries
3rd	1972–76	8.0%	10.1%	45.5%	Export industries, self sufficiency in food
4th	1977–81	8.0%	5.6%	20.2%	Heavy industries, technology-intensive industries
5th	1982–86	7.5%	–	–	Social welfare, information-based industries

In the first FYEP, the government chose to foster import-substitution industries such as food processing, fertilisers and oil refining, and to develop the basic infrastructure. As domestic savings were almost non existent, the government relied heavily on foreign loans to finance these projects. In 1968 and 1970, the country's first two major highways were opened, which brought the entire nation into a single-day economic zone.

As the economy became capable of providing for the basic needs of the people, the government redirected its goals in the second FYEP to expanding exports. To provide impetus for export growth, the government introduced a number of incentives: subsidies in the form of export loans; tariff exemptions for imported raw materials and accelerated depreciation for spare parts; reduced rates on public utilities; and the president's personal attention with awards for achievement. The emphasis was on textiles and other light industries, because these labour-intensive processes could absorb large numbers of unemployed and turn them into a well-disciplined and internationally competitive labour force.

The third FYEP continued to emphasise export expansion and added agricultural development. The *Saemaul* (new village) programme was started in 1970, which provided villagers with assistance in building roads, bridges, irrigation networks, reservoirs and water distribution systems. The result was rapid rural development, transforming Korea from a major rice importer to a rice exporter in 1977. By 1980, average family income in the rural areas matched that in the city.

The oil shock of 1973 shook Korea's economic recovery. At the time, 53.5 percent of the nation's total energy requirements were supplied by oil, all of which had to be imported. The cost of oil rose from less than $300 million in 1972 to over $1 billion in 1974, representing 14.9 percent of total imports (Figure 7.2). The added burden increased Korea's chronic balance of payments deficit in 1974 to $2.4 billion and endangered the economic solvency of the nation.

While most other countries were holding their breath in the wake of the 1973 oil crisis and the worldwide recession which accompanied it, the Korean government chose to encourage the expansion and upgrading of production facilities. This policy and its timing allowed Korean companies to purchase technology, plant and equipment at bargain prices in a buyer's market.

At the same time, Korean businessmen rapidly moved to the Middle East, winning contracts for construction works and selling Korean goods. By 1976, the Korean balance of trade with the Middle East was in parity. Korean businessmen also found ways to overcome Western protectionism: first by responding to limits on the volume of imports with increased value-added per item; and second by diversifying its export markets to other parts of the world (Figure 7.3). Established in 1975, general trading companies became a major vehicle for export growth. By 1983, the combined exports of nine general trading companies amounted to 51 percent of the Korean total (Table 7.2).

Encouraged by its success, the government felt the time was ripe to invest in chemicals and heavy industries and directed the fourth FYEP accordingly. Economically, Korea needed to move from textiles and light industry because of rising wages and increasing competition from less developed countries. The new goals also resulted from military pressures. North Korea's continuing threats coupled with President Carter's decision to withdraw US military forces from Korea meant the country had to develop defence-related industries.

Seoul, the capital and business centre of Korea, was located just 30 miles south of the Demilitarised Zone. Frequent border incidents took place almost daily, and experts estimated that the North had the military advantage in spite of the fact the South spent six percent of its GNP, or close to 40 percent of its budget, on defence.

By the late 1970s, Korea's economic recovery was

Figure 7.2: Composition of imports

A. By Commodity

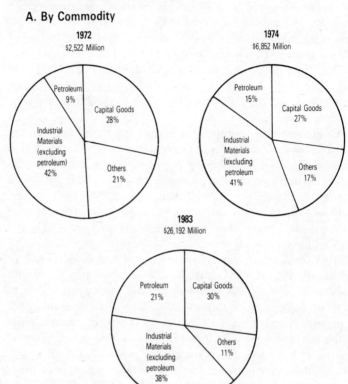

1972
$2,522 Million

1974
$6,852 Million

1983
$26,192 Million

B. By Region

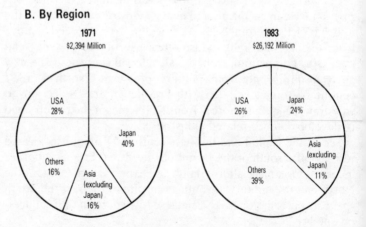

1971
$2,394 Million

1983
$26,192 Million

Source: Trade Yearbook (Korea Trade Association, 1982), pp. 423–32.

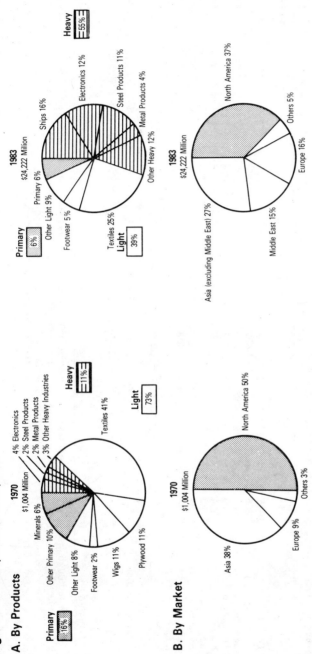

Figure 7.3: Composition of exports

A. By Products

1970
$1,004 Million

Primary 16%
Heavy 11%
Light 73%

4% Electronics
2% Steel Products
2% Metal Products
3% Other Heavy Industries
Textiles 41%
Minerals 6%
Other Primary 10%
Other Light 8%
Footwear 2%
Wigs 11%
Plywood 11%

1983
$24,222 Million

Primary 6%
Heavy 55%
Light 39%

Electronics 12%
Steel Products 11%
Metal Products 4%
Other Heavy 12%
Ships 16%
Primary 6%
Other Light 9%
Footwear 5%
Textiles 25%

B. By Market

1970
$1,004 Million

North America 50%
Others 3%
Europe 9%
Asia 38%

1983
$24,222 Million

North America 37%
Others 5%
Europe 16%
Middle East 15%
Asia (excluding Middle East) 27%

Note: The export year for 1983 was from 1 November 1982 to 31 October 1983.
Sources: 1970 data – Trade Yearbook (Korea Trade Association, 1982), pp. 304–313.
1983 data – Hankook – Kyongje – Shinamoon, 1 December 1983, p. 2

87

Table 7.2: Exports of the nine general trading companies[a]

($ millions)

Company	1975	1976	1977	1978	1979	1980	1981	1982	1983	1984 (Planned)
Samsung	205	333	390	492	772	1,237	1,607	1,860	2,205	2,800
Daewoo	138	259	362	706	1,120	1,415	1,914	1,971	2,513	3,000
Ssangyong	106	101	117	264	422	650	756	971	1,035	1,050
Kukje	64	194	297	472	564	745	849	834	861	1,000
Sunkyong	52	107	176	283	322	421	585	601	661	920
Hyosung	34	106	153	338	582	761	787	599	687	900
Kumho	32	78	135	256	305	357	185	166	178	206
Lucky-Goldstar[b]	31	134	199	330	469	493	619	689	1,065	1,250
Hyundai[c]	–	–	323	260	493	1,028	1,721	2,667	3,133	3,500
General trading company total	662	1,312	2,152	3,402	5,050	7,117	9,043	10,458	12,358	14,626
National total	5,081	7,715	10,047	12,711	15,056	17,505	21,254	21,616	24,222	27,000
General trading company share (%)	13.0	17.0	21.4	26.8	33.5	40.7	42.5	48.4	51.0	54.2

Notes: [a] Although there were 10 General Trading Companies in Korea, Korea International Company was excluded from the listing here because it was a small government-held and operated company providing export services to small companies.
[b] Bando Sanga changed its name to Lucky-Goldstar on 1st January 1984.
[c] Hyundai General Trading Company was established in 1977, and thus had no export activities in 1975 and 1976.

experiencing serious problems. One was the inflationary impact of the investments in chemicals and heavy industries. Since the positive effects of these investments on the economy would take years to materialise, the government came under pressure to print money as a stopgap measure. In 1977 and 1978, money supply (M2) increased by 37 percent and 39 percent. The wholesale price index, in turn, rose 18.8 percent and 38.9 percent in 1979 and 1980.

Excess capacity soon became another serious problem. The large companies had rushed to take advantage of the incentives offered for investment in chemicals and heavy industry. The domestic market was not large enough to absorb the volume of these new plants needed to break even on costs, so that when world markets shrank as a result of a deepening global recession, plant utilisation plummeted. For example, plant capacity utilisation in the new machinery sector dropped from 74 percent in late 1977 to 35 percent in 1980.

The emphasis on heavy industry was at the expense of the light industry, which continued to be the foreign currency breadwinner. As a result, export growth slowed down. Another oil shock in 1979 and the resulting increase in international interest rates led to a critical shortage of foreign reserves. As the economy was running into trouble, the head of the Korean CIA assassinated President Park. The ensuing political chaos threatened further woe.

The new government under President Chun set out to change the economic emphasis from rapid 'expansion at the expense of inflation' to more equitable income distribution and increased education, health and social expenditure. To reflect these new policies, the new plan was named the Fifth Five-Year Economic and Social Development Plan.

Export-led growth was still at the heart of the plan, but the strategies were different to the previous ones. The plan directed attention to the upgrading of light industry, so that small and medium-sized companies should receive more support. The problem sectors in heavy industry were to be consolidated, and government support limited to those areas in which Korea could be internationally competitive. By late 1983, the heavy industries, shipbuilding and automobile sectors had begun to recover.

The government saw growing worldwide protectionism as one of the most serious threats to Korea's future development and growth. One response, under the leadership of Dr Kim Jae-Ik, a

Stanford-educated economist who served as chief economic advisor to the president of Korea, was to remove protectionist policies in Korea. He took the position that the major Korean firms had to learn to compete if they were to become effective in building Korea's economic power. Although not everyone agreed, the strongest opposition was with respect to timing. In the view of these opponents, the government was trying to move too quickly; the removal of government support and protection should be implemented slowly and selectively. Dr Kim Jae-Ik disagreed, and saw his policies in liberalisation prevail as the principal blueprint for industrial development. In late October 1983, following Dr Kim's death in the Rangoon bombing, the newly appointed chief economic advisor Dr Sakong Il, pledged his intention to continue his predecessor's economic policies.

PRESSURES FROM ABROAD

In 1984, Korea faced increasing pressure from US officials to reduce its trade surplus with the United States and to make Korean markets more accessible to American goods and services. In March 1984, a Korean buying mission placed $3.2 billion of orders for American products. This action represented a Korean commitment to restructure trade patterns by increasing purchases from the US at the expense of Japan. *The Wall Street Journal* reported on the event as follows:

> 'We have a severe trade deficit with Japan and a big trade surplus with the US, so this could solve both problems,' says Leu Byong Hion, Seoul's ambassador to Washington. 'We're happy with the business but redressing the trade balance misses the point,' a State Department official says. 'Market access is more important.'

Asked in an interview reported in the monthly economic and trade publication, *Business Korea* (July 1984), if Korea's new policies of economic liberalisation were happening because of foreign pressure, Dr Sakong responded:

> We have liberalized and internationalized our economy because it's good for us. Since our market is relatively large here and we are growing very fast, many countries are

interested in Korea as a potential market. Of course, they would like to see our economy open up. Outside pressure however, is not a major reason for our liberalisation efforts.

With respect to outside pressures, some observers questioned the intensity of US demands on Korea to liberalise trade in view of its relatively small surplus ($1.8 billion) compared to those of Japan (over $20 billion) and Taiwan ($7 billion).

LEADING BUSINESS GROUPS

The growth of the Korean economy was accompanied by the increasing prominence of the large business groups known as *Chaebol*. Nine Korean companies were included in *Fortune's* list of the 500 largest industrial corporations outside the United States (Table 7.3). Only six countries — Japan, the United Kingdom, West Germany, France, Canada and Italy — had more companies among the top 250. Of the country's ten major firms, only one was government-owned. This reflected the government's early decision to harness private initiative as a principal means of economic growth.

Hyundai, Daewoo, Samsung and Lucky-Goldstar groups stand out because of their size and diversification. The four groups had followed different strategies but their business portfolios were quite similar and they each competed in most of the important industrial sectors.

Chaebol *under fire*

Representative of the mounting public criticism against big business groups was an article in *Business Korea* (July 1984), which cited several alleged financial abuses in its attack on *Chaebol*:

> Many of the heavy corporate debtors are major shareholders in banks in addition to their holdings in other less important financial institutions, giving rise to public criticism that *Chaebol* borrow from banks to buy control of banks.
>
> Sometimes *Chaebol* acquire equity free of any financing burden. The simplest version of this is for two subsidiaries of a

Table 7.3: Ten largest industrial corporations, 1982

Rank	Company	Sales $ million	Assets $ million	Net Income $ million	Equity $ million	Employees
1 (41)[a]	Hyundai	8,036	6,069	108	1,141	137,000
2 (62)	Sunkyong	6,270	2,485	27	312	17,832
3 (65)	Daewoo[b]	6,060	5,738	46[d]	714	70,000
4 (67)	Samsung	5,967	4,641	28	709	97,384
5 (82)	Lucky-Goldstar	5,461	3,666	74	595	42,752
6 (161)	Ssangyong	2,892	2,293	19	297	16,818
7 (206)	Pohang Iron & Steel[c]	2,383	4,155	21	1,779	14,473
8 (236)	Korea Explosives	2,074	1,923	17	305	17,091
9 (238)	Hyosung	2,061	1,855	1	334	20,878
10 (247)	Kukje	1,992	1,495	7	87	41,800

Notes: [a] Ranking on *Fortune*'s listing of the 500 largest industrial corporations outside the US.
[b] Since Daewoo did not report its results to *Fortune*, company data were used to compare it with the others.
[c] Among the ten largest corporations listed, only Pohang Iron & Steel Corporation (POSCO) was not privately held.
[d] Before tax.

Source: *Fortune*, 22nd August 1983, pp. 172–81.

group to pingpong investment between each other for a minimum-cost, or even cost-free nominal capital build up.

Last year, 128 company-to-company equity deals were reported and 77 percent of these took place between subsidiaries of a group. Under the zero-sum scheme, one of the *Chaebol* has raised its four subsidiaries' net combined capital 3.5 times, from 4 billion Won to 14 billion Won.

The chief attraction of the zero-sum game is that generally a company qualifies for as much credit as is determined by the company's capital size, real or nominal. A nominal increase in capital also decreases the profit-to-capital ratio and may help distract the attentive eye of the price authority.

The *Chaebol* were also criticised for their rapid growth and the resulting increased market concentration. The *Business Korea* article noted, 'From 1977 to 1981, the five front runners increased their combined turnover from 14.8 percent of the industry total to 21.5 percent, while reducing employment from 8.5 percent to 8.4 percent.'

In defence of such concentration and growth, Mr Chung Ju Yung, chairman of the Hyundai business group and chairman of the Federation of Korean Industries argued that, 'Large Korean corporations competing with corporations of the United States, Japan and other advanced countries, are nothing but the world economy's kindergarten children in terms of sales and profits.'

8

Economic Policy

Jin Nyum

SUMMARY

Mr Jin, who describes himself as a 'working-level' economist, analyses the economic problems facing Korea. He describes the supportive role taken by government as well as its determination to liberalise trade and promote small and medium-sized high technology companies.

Current areas of concern include the country's need to grow sufficiently to provide jobs, and the rising expectations of all Koreans, especially those on low incomes. Mr Jin also discusses the Sixth Economic and Social Plan, and emphasises that the government will continue to respond to changes in the world economic environment.

Economic growth in 1985 has not been as promising as hoped. Growth of GNP for the first half of 1985 was only three to four percent, far below expectations; nor has the balance of payments improved substantially.

From the beginning of the year, the government foresaw that the country's export performance would be disappointing. As a result, we introduced a comprehensive package to improve export competitiveness and promote investment in selected manufacturing sectors. As policies take time to become fully effective, we were happy to see increasing signs of economic improvement by the beginning in the third quarter.

The government is still determined to adopt a wait-and-see stance on the effects of its policy proposals. Estimated GNP for the third quarter of the year shows 5.4 percent growth over the same period last year. The balance of payments, at the end of

94

September 1985, showed a $700 million deficit, which got worse in October.

It will require prudent economic policies to merely maintain the projected deficit in the balance of payments for 1985. The government so far is confident it can keep increases to about three percent in consumer prices and perhaps about one percent in wholesale prices over 1984, in spite of poor results in the agricultural sector. We think price stabilisation may be more difficult to maintain in 1986. For the past year, we have been fortunate that the prices of raw materials have tended to be stable, with decreases balancing gains. International institutes and government projections indicate a rising trend in the price movement on international raw materials. If this materialises, we shall have to put more emphasis on price stabilisation during 1986.

Economic growth for 1986 will depend on other countries, and especially on the development of protectionist practices, tariff and non-tariff in nature. Our tentative projection regarding exports in 1986 is eight to nine percent overall growth — six percent in real terms but eight or nine percent if adjusted for price changes.

The government aims to achieve a balance on current account by 1986, which means we must increase exports and economise on imports. At the same time, we realise that we must improve our domestic savings effort in order to finance our total investment.

I am often asked, especially by foreign businessmen, what balancing the current account means to the Korean economy. Our answer is that we must concentrate our efforts on reducing the huge balance of payments deficit, which is the fourth highest in the world. We do not believe we have a serious problem in servicing the debt, especially if we are successful in controlling inflation for three or four consecutive years and maintain the projection of $2,000 GNP per capita. If we stimulate more domestic savings, especially personal savings, we shall be able to finance investment by ourselves.

At the same time, because the economy faces chronic balance of payments problems, the government has limited options in promoting growth and employment. If we can balance our current account for two or three years, we will be able to utilise a second 'engine of growth' in addition to exports. A balanced current account should also solve the so-called devaluation problems, because the government would be in a better position to persuade the Korean people of the necessity and justice of devaluation.

For 1986 the government is concentrating on export and investment promotion programmes to improve growth. The target for 1986 is six to seven percent growth, a three percent rise in consumer prices, and a current account almost in balance.

The economy is in a state of transition. Both industry and the economy are sensitive to developments in other industrialised and developing countries. We face protectionist practices in the industrialised nations and heavier competition from the labour-intensive industries of the developing countries. The major problems we must solve are how to meet the ever-increasing expectations of the Korean people and, at the same time, cope with ever-changing international trade and economic environments.

The government's plans over the next three to four years are, first of all, to promote reliance on market forces. The government has already been trying to deregulate and lessen government intervention, especially in the private sector, but we have more to do. The government will continue to give the private sector a freer hand in the conduct of its own business. At the same time, it will strengthen its role in income distribution and social welfare. A country with only $2,000 per capita GNP is not able to improve its social services to equal those of more developed countries. But we should pay more attention, for example, to creating job opportunities for young people and improving the institutional frameworks, especially for lower-income groups.

Another challenge arises from employment. Although overall unemployment is not too high, the employment absorption ratio has been deteriorating. For example, in the 1960s and 1970s, one percent growth would provide 50 to 60 thousand jobs. Seven percent growth should be able to provide young people with 400 thousand jobs. In practice, one percent growth absorbs fewer than 40 thousand people. Companies are trying to cut expenditure and improve productivity. That means, at least in the short run, that they are cutting down on manpower.

Attempts to promote new investment, especially in the manufacturing sector and in small and medium-sized companies have not been very successful, so the government has been thinking about introducing special incentives for investment in the medium-sized companies, especially in the technology-intensive areas. Plans covering deregulation, and a tax-free period for three years following the establishment of a business are likely to begin early in 1986.

Resources will be allocated to provide more help for lower-income groups. In order to ease unemployment, we are developing better labour-information support programmes. We aim to balance the current account by next year and to continue to liberalise trade. Despite criticism that we are slow in opening up our markets, we are doing our best, not only for the sake of other countries, but for the good of our own economy. The problem is that some overseas markets are closing, but over the next three to four years, we will co-operate with developed and developing countries to expand world trade.

I have not been too definite in my explanation of our economic programmes but as I explained earlier they are now under intensive study. Further ideas and projections will be finalised by the end of this year. After the final draft of the Sixth Economic and Social Plan is completed at the end of this year, it will be debated over the first half of next year.

QUESTIONS AND ANSWERS

What is the forecast for growth?
Preliminary studies suggest growth potential for the next four to five years at an annual rate of about eight percent. A minimum of seven percent is needed to provide jobs. But an economy such as ours is dependent on world trade; we can not grow alone, without considering changes in the international economic environment.

Are there adequate managerial skills in the small and medium-sized companies?
That is one of the big problems we have to solve. Because some of these industries have had no access to graduates, we have been trying to expand managerial support programmes for them. Managerial and marketing skills are crucial to us today. We have improved facilities and are developing a framework for training manpower. We also encourage people who have worked in large companies to set up on their own.

It is difficult, if not impossible, for a foreign firm to take over a Korean company. Wouldn't it dramatically stimulate foreign investment and the creation of jobs, if the rules for foreign companies to acquire a majority or minority position in Korean firms were simplified?

The government's strategy is to provide freer opportunities for foreign investors to do business. We have strong manufacturing capabilities but face severe problems in technology transfer. Our strategy is to combine foreign technology with local manufacturing. Once that strategy is established, if there still are barriers to the acquisition of Korean firms I shall want to check and see, and then do my best to put things right.

Would you comment on the government's policy on wage increases?

This is a difficult area for the government at present. Blue-collar workers especially are on low incomes. The problem is how to reconcile two conflicting goals: stabilisation of real incomes and enlargement of job opportunities, particularly in labour-intensive industries. Up to last year, we had explicit wage guidelines. This year, the private sector is encouraged to decide rates for themselves.

The blue-collar unions in particular are complaining about wages and asking for rapid, across-the-board adjustments. Next spring, we expect to face the same situation again. Our policy is to persuade managers and employees to see the real situation and together try to stabilise wages. Very difficult —but we must do it.

These days, employment is not good, which means that the feeling is spreading, even amongst employees, that it is more prudent to reach a settlement. We are trying to set up cooperative procedures over wages for next year.

Are there government plans to intervene over exchange rates?

The government is not in a position to manipulate exchange rates. However, the drop in value of the past five or six months between the dollar and other currencies has allowed the government to float the Won. At the moment, both the government and the central bank feel the present level of the Won is affecting our trading relations. However, we have avoided manipulating the Won to promote exports or curtail imports. That kind of policy, we feel, would have a short-term impact but not be beneficial in the long run.

To sum up, Korean policies will remain flexible and adjust to both external and internal conditions. The central goals of following market forces, of liberalisation, stability and efficiency will remain. The Korean government will continue to work with both domestic and foreign business for the mutual benefit of us all.

9

Korean–American Economic Relations

George G.B. Griffin

SUMMARY

Mr Griffin defends US trade policy as perhaps the most liberal among industrialised nations, and stresses the commitment of the Reagan Administration to an open international trading system, despite the political reality of protectionism and its dangers. His two main points are that Korea has grown beyond the status of an infant economy, and that the country is a major player on the international scene in too many areas to ignore the responsibilities that come with that status.

Over the last two decades, Korea has produced one of the world's most successful economies. Korea's output has grown from about $100 per capita in 1961 to about $2,000 in 1984. Progress in quality of life factors such as education, health, construction of new roads and housing has equalled economic growth.

Throughout these two decades, the primary engine of growth for Korea's development has been exports, as Korea pursued an outward-looking economic strategy. The American domestic market has been the largest single market for Korean exports and a major source of Korean imports. There has been a sustained pattern of annual growth and a rough balance in the bilateral trade volume during this period. As a result, Korea is now America's seventh largest trading partner (ahead of France and Italy) and the fifth largest market for American agricultural products. The bilateral trading relationship continues to grow; in 1984, the US received 36 percent of Korea's exports and 22 percent of Korea's imports were from the US. In recent years, however, the bilateral trade balance shifted dramatically in Korea's favour, causing trade frictions and frustrations for both America and Korea.

The revolution of economic development which has occurred in Korea over the past 25 years is an event which could be compared in its significance to the Industrial Revolution in Western Europe. The major impetus to this impressive economic growth has been international trade and the United States has been a major participant in that trade. To understand the dynamic progress of Korea, it is appropriate to examine American trade policy and Korea's trade relations with the United States.

HISTORICAL CONTEXT OF US-KOREAN BILATERAL TRADE

The most distinctive feature of American trade policy over the past 50 years has been liberalisation. Through a series of bilateral and multilateral negotiations, US tariffs have decreased steadily to about 20 percent of their average level in 1930. However, as with policy formulation in any country, there have been shifts and adjustments — ebbs and flows, if you will — in the nature and extent of the support for trade liberalisation. Trade liberalisation in the first half of this century was influenced by a range of important political and economic factors in the thinking of American society of that time. Foremost among these was the reorientation of trade goals in the post-World War Two period from promoting broad political and security goals of the United States to, as we have seen in recent years, advancing national economic objectives and responding to domestic political pressures based on special economic interests. Another significant influence during this period has been the increase of non-tariff measures to regulate international trade while actual tariffs have been reduced drastically.

Long before the end of World War Two, US foreign policy leaders concluded that the lack of an open world economy during the 1930s, symbolised by the highly protectionist Smoot-Hawley Act, greatly contributed to the outbreak of the war. They encouraged President Roosevelt to take the lead in establishing an international free market system to promote stable economic as well as political systems. Thus, even before the end of World War Two, the Roosevelt Administration not only drafted a

101

proposal for a multilateral trade organisation but also requested from Congress substantial new tariff-reducing powers. President Truman eventually succeeded in achieving authority to cut tariffs, but not the authority to establish a multilateral trade organisation. Even these efforts met with considerable opposition from powerful interests which wanted to close the US market to imports.

In response to these protectionist pressures, President Truman in 1947 issued an executive order establishing a formal escape clause procedure which permitted the modification or withdrawal of tariff reductions when increased imports caused or threatened to cause serious injury to an industry. The escape-clause measure is an indication that US commitment at this time was to a policy of liberal rather than free trade. American policy makers recognised that protection of a few industries might be necessary if they were injured seriously by increased imports.

Nevertheless, the implementation of the change from the inward-looking policies pursued by most countries in the 1930s and 1940s to a liberal international trade regime was progressive and required the support of other countries in addition to the United States.

The necessity for international support is relevant to the theme of this seminar. It demonstrates how and to what extent Korea has been able to take advantage of the economic benefits of a liberal international market place. It also shows how Korea's participation benefits Korean and other businesses alike.

I would argue that an open international trading system is a general public benefit. For example, if one country reduces tariffs under the 'most favoured nation' principle, other countries benefit from the improved export opportunities even if they do not make reciprocal cuts in duties themselves. As a consequence, there is an incentive for any country to try for a free ride by taking advantage of reductions of trade barriers in other countries.

When countries fail to share the responsibilities as well as the benefits of a free market system, balanced multilateral tariff reductions do not occur even though it would be to the advantage of all. Some countries limit themselves to short-term benefits even when it can be demonstrated that a balanced, multilateral reduction in duties would be to their long-term advantage. On the other hand, from an economic perspective, if one country's position is strong compared to that of the others, such as

America's was, the cost to that nation of free rides by others is sometimes outweighed by improvements in the world economy. By practising such a benign policy, the strong member may encourage less economically powerful nations to practise reciprocity.

In the immediate post-World War Two period, the United States was willing and able to bear most of the costs of establishing a liberal international economic order. Other major industrial countries were plagued by balance of payments problems and rationed foreign exchange for their reconstruction efforts. As a result, tariff concessions they made in early multilateral negotiations were not very meaningful in terms of increasing US exports. US negotiators were fully aware of this, but none the less several times offered greater tariff concessions than they received, by usual measures of recipocity. In effect, the United States carried out a plan to redistribute to other countries part of the surplus generated by its stronger economy. This was done to convince other countries to support the establishment of an open trading system. However, recent detrimental changes in the trading position of the United States compared to most countries have caused our decision makers to re-evaluate American trade policy.

Beginning in the 1960s, America's relative economic power began to decline. The US share of merchandise exports of the 15 largest industrial economies fell from 25.2 percent in 1960 to 20.5 percent in 1970 and further to 18.3 percent in 1979. The US share of exports of manufactured items for the same years are 22.8 percent, 18.4 percent, and 15.5 percent respectively.

In the 1950s and 1960s the industrial countries continued to reduce tariffs and began to focus on the trade distortions inherent in non-tariff barriers. They began to understand that quantity restrictions, export rebates, and domestic subsidies could nullify the benefits of trade liberalisation. However, in the late 1960s increased use of non-tariff barriers stemmed not only from the efforts of particular industries to gain protection or special export assistance, but also from government concern over balance of payments problems and various social and economic policy objectives. To counter this new trend, the US government began to negotiate agreements aimed at mitigating the adverse effects of foreign non-tariff barriers. In spite of some progress in this area, it is obvious that the increased use of non-tariff, trade distorting measures continue to weaken the free market system by encouraging protectionism and legitimising arrangements outside the GATT framework.

CURRENT US–KOREAN TRADE

All post-World War Two US presidents have supported the free market system. None has been more firm in his belief in the economic advantages of liberal trade than President Reagan. His Administration's stance on trade issues was set forth officially by then-United States Trade Representative William Brock in July 1981. In his Statement on US Trade Policy, Ambassador Brock maintained that free trade is essential to a strong US economy. At the same time, he emphasised that the Reagan Administration would strictly enforce US laws and international agreements relating to unfair practices such as dumping and government subsidies. Current Reagan Administration policy is to keep US markets open and press other governments to reduce or eliminate measures which artificially stimulate exports or block imports.

Most of the Administration's policies aimed at providing relief from injury caused by import competition have been shaped by free trade ideology. On the basis of Mr Brock's Statement on US Trade Policy, an observer of the Reagan Administration would expect a tough posture against increased imports. This has not been the case; actual instances of granting import protection have been few. Given the political constraints within which the President and Congress operate and the strong protectionist pressures produced by the trade-distorting measures of foreign governments, Washington's record in free trade remains relatively liberal. Instead of raising trade barriers, the US government has relied on enforcement of its fair trade laws and negotiations for greater access to foreign markets for US exporters.

In recent years, the main push for stricter enforcement of US laws relating to practices by foreign countries such as dumping subsidies, patent infringements, and unjustifiable, unreasonable or discriminatory trade factors has come from Congress. In 1979 Congress transferred the authority to enforce fair trade laws from the Treasury to the Department of Commerce. However, i is under the Reagan Administration that fair trade laws have been enforced most stringently.

Throughout the Reagan Administration, and especially in recent months, US trade officials have been vigorous in demanding fairness in trade between the US and other countries. No trade topic generates more heated discussion in Washington than the US trade deficit with Japan, and there is great concern that other countries may follow Japan's example. I am sure Koreans perceive the frustration building in the US over the widening US trade gap and lack of access to foreign markets, Korea included.

Another issue of serious concern is intellectual property rights. Protection of copyrights, patents and trademarks has been the subject of three new American trade laws in recent months. The new laws and heightened interest spurred by recent studies prepared by a Presidential Commission and Congressional committees will make intellectual property matters extremely prominent in future trade negotiations and trade disputes. For example, under the 1984 US Trade Act, continuation of GSP benefits is linked closely with a developing country's adherence to meaningful protection of American intellectual property.

The most serious threat today to the world economy, including the domestic economies of the US and Korea, is protectionism. Protectionist measures usually invite a spiral of retaliation. Even when there is no immediate retaliation, or trade war, protectionism fosters inefficient uses of a nation's resources and raises the cost of living. A favoured industry may benefit initially from a quota, subsidy or other trade-distorting measure, but eventually greater and greater costs are borne by the people of the nation protecting its industries and markets.

Protectionism manifests itself in many forms: tariffs, surveillance, subsidies, unnecessary licensing, or recommendation by industry associations, to name just a few. A protectionist measure is usually invoked to provide an adjustment period for an industry to modernise and become more competitive. The theory is that soon it will be able to stand on its own, with no artificial support, after which protection will be eliminated. Unfortunately, the opposite is usually the case. Not only do barriers obviate the need for the protected industry to become more efficient, but they also attract more resources into a sector which probably already has excess capacity. Korea, even more than the US, has a great stake in preserving and extending the open trading system. Korea does not have America's huge internal market, nor its abundant natural resources. In 1984, a substantial proportion (about 37 percent) of Korea's GNP came from exports. This is reflected in current Korean government policies which continue to emphasise increased exports to sustain economic growth. The Korean government recognizes that trade restrictions can quickly upset the economic equilibrium necessary to promote economic progress for both our countries.

As might be expected, more realistic behaviour by the US in its international economic relations has resulted in an increased number of trade frictions between the United States and other countries. Many who support a liberal trading order are concerned that new strictures and retaliations will become so pervasive and difficult to solve that the world trading system will collapse as nations pursue inward-looking protectionist policies. This is, of course, a possibility.

When countries go beyond the intent of the rules and engage in beggar thy neighbour policies, in effect transferring or exporting unemployment and economic problems to another country, the free market system can suffer severe damage. Many historians and other observers are convinced that such policies triggered the tensions that caused World War Two. At the same time, others take hope from a perception that current disagreements do not involve the principles of an open trading system, but simply interpretations of those principles.

FUTURE US–KOREAN TRADE

Future US trade policy will be influenced by the reluctance from a political viewpoint of any American president to promote openly a policy of protectionism. The United States is viewed by other major industrial nations as the leader of the liberal international trading order which developed after World War Two. These countries still support, at least theoretically, an open trading system and believe that if the United States adopts general protectionism, it will spread rapidly throughout the world.

On the other hand, it also will be very difficult for an American president to resist granting some protection to specific industries which are politically significant. Thus, we may see a more aggressive US approach to mitigate unemployment and create higher income levels through international trade. More broadly, future US presidents will likely strive to insure that GATT rules are enforced properly, so that international trading practices do not continue to work to the disadvantage of the United States.

Despite great attention and efforts from Washington, the overall US trade deficit is growing larger. Current statistics reveal that America's imports are growing faster than her economic growth. They are displacing US production at an accelerating rate. These surging imports have intensified demands for protection from a host of industries which are losing jobs and markets to foreign competitors. To date, the Reagan Administration has been able to uphold its free-trade principles in the face of mounting political pressures. How long that stand can be maintained will depend in large part on how successful we are in attacking protectionism elsewhere and how quickly we can reduce America's balance of trade deficit.

Many trade specialists are accepting a new economic theory which contends that international competitors in low-wage countries are causing the de-industrialisation of America. They point to a reduction in the standards of living among US industrial workers, and the loss of US sales and jobs in a wide range of products, including steel, autos, machinery, textiles and electronics. Some policy makers argue that there are grave dangers to free trade since high-income countries cannot compete successfully with low-income countries for jobs and sales of goods and services.

The Reagan Administration has begun to take a more active, problem-solving approach to mounting trade pressures. To the extent that this strategy improves US export performance, it will also reduce protectionist pressure. For this reason, current Administration actions should not be viewed as protectionist. In fact, they are specifically aimed at keeping US trade barriers down by helping to alleviate the cause of protectionist sentiment.

US Trade Representative Clayton Yeutter, while stopping short of abandoning free market trade policies, recently told the Senate Finance Committee that turning the other cheek on trade issues has cost the US dearly, both in import competition and in export difficulties. In response to Congressional demands to act more forcefully in response to complaints from manufacturers, Yeutter has agreed to provide import relief when necessary to particularly hard-hit industries. But it is clear that neither Yeutter nor any other trade official wants Congress to resolve America's industrial and unemployment problems through legislation.

Korea's reliance on trade, especially its exports to the US, as a way to stimulate growth gives American trade policy adjustments a critical meaning. How can Korea best deal with the challenges to its development these policy developments may bring? By assuming more of the responsibilities inherent in its international trade role, Korea can offer more market potential to developed countries and expect in return better access to their markets.

With its large, well educated and growing middle class population, Korea represents a potentially important market for American exports of goods and services. Business leaders in the US are keen to maintain an appropriate share of this rapidly growing market and to increase their range of exports. Seoul's willingness to lower import barriers and offer equitable conditions for them to do business would provide significant bargaining power. In return, US trade policy officials could justify keeping American markets open to Korean goods. Korea has grown beyond the status of an infant economy and is capable of causing serious injury to American industry. This could be moderated if reciprocity in market access is practised.

I am sure Korean trade officials realise that what is done in Seoul or Ulsan is of consequence to Americans living in the industrial centres and small towns of the US, just as policies made in Washington affect Korean manufacturers and exporters. We think it is important for Korea to assume the influence and responsibilities which it has earned by its important position as the world's thirteenth largest trading nation. Bilateral economic adjustments are an indication of a dynamic economic relationship which presents new challenges and opportunities. Washington officials are well aware of the security and economic development problems Korea faces. Nevertheless, Korea is a major player on the international scene in too many areas to ignore the responsibilities that come with that status. Korean exports of steel, shipbuilding, footwear, textiles and electronics, to name just a few, when supported by trade disruptive practices such as subsidies, dumping or illegal preferential financing, are just one aspect of the problem. More importantly, the realities of economic difficulties and consequent political reactions in the US demand that Korea take action to improve market access and intellectual property protection without fail and without delay. The international market place of the late 1980s will not sit by and wait for Korea to follow Japan's liberalisation model. To avoid becoming fully identified with Japan and the problems it is causing in the US, I expect Korea will continue to liberalise access to its market, and to act in the international arena with the maturity it has displayed in building its modern economy.

The international trading system which has served both the US and Korea so well is under fierce attack. Korea's economic success could not have occurred without the multilateral trade liberalisation which began in 1960 with the GATT Kennedy Round. Worldwide tariff rates have been reduced drastically, and many subsidy practices, non-tariff barriers and other forms of protection are now governed by international rules.

There are still challenges ahead. Of highest priority is the development of new rules to govern policies which restrict the flow of technology, services and investment. Restricted access to markets, a lack of protection of intellectual and industrial property, inconsistent and opaque investment and import regulations, and constant 'renegotiation' of contract terms, all discourage new investments in capital and the transfer of technology.

We are at a critical point in international trading history. Governments can increase manipulation of their nations' economies, or they can build prosperity on open competition and on reciprocal market access. The biggest challenge is to coordinate political and economic goals. To keep the world trading system open, business must get out from behind artificial barriers and renew its commitment to unfettered competition as the engine of growth. This is as important to Korea as it is to the US.

Index